PERFORMANCE DRIVEN LEADERSHIP

Forging High-Performance Teams Through Communication, Coaching, and Culture

ERIC ZICHTERMAN

Published by: Executive Books | Tremendous Life Books

P.O. Box 267, Boiling Springs, PA 17007
717-701-8159 | 800-233-2665

www.TremendousLeadership.com

Paperback ISBN: 978-1-961202-74-0
eBook ISBN: 978-1-961202-75-7

CONTENTS

ABOUT THE AUTHOR

My name is Eric Zichterman, and I grew up in Cedar Rapids, Iowa. My first job was at my uncle's hotel and convention center. Working in hospitality shaped my understanding of Customer Experience—what many call Customer Service. Managing close to 40 hours per week throughout high school, often on nights and weekends, instilled a strong work ethic in me. I quickly learned that success requires continuous effort—no one hands it to you.

As graduation neared, I was uncertain about my next move. After the Easter and Mother's Day rush at the hotel, I assisted a small concrete contracting company where my brother worked. The owner, Chad, was exceptionally diligent and dedicated; his approach to work deeply influenced me. Over the next 11 years, I worked beside Chad, gaining firsthand experience in construction. The daily sense of accomplishment I felt was profound—something difficult to fully describe to others.

After more than a decade in concrete contracting, I spent two years working for a large General Contractor (GC) as a Concrete Superintendent. However, after working most of my twenties from sun-up to sun-down, the 7:00 AM to 3:30 PM schedule at the GC firm didn't suit me. I wasn't wired for that, I needed more. I soon transitioned into a Project Manager role with a Heavy Highway Civil

Earthwork and Utility Contractor looking to expand into the concrete market. Under Craig's mentorship, I gained extensive knowledge of job costing, project management, estimating, and operational systems. However, the most valuable lesson Craig taught me was not to sweat the small stuff. Coming from the high-intensity, fast-paced concrete industry of the Midwest, where 100-degree summer days could lead to flaring tempers, this wisdom became a guiding principle in both my professional and personal life.

Eventually, I decided it was time to start my own company. This led to a difficult but pivotal conversation with my wife; I told her I planned to launch a concrete business. At the time, we had a three-year-old and a nine-month-old, and her response was the one I'll never forget: "Are you kidding me right now? We have two small children to take care of." Rather than discouraging me, her words fueled my motivation for success. So, in the middle of summer, far from an ideal time, we opened our doors. Thanks to the relationships and industry connections I had built over the years, I secured enough work to have a strong start, setting the foundation for a business that thrived.

In 2017, I joined a business peer group of construction professionals, a decision that proved invaluable. The collective wisdom of this group, many of whom remain close friends today, played a crucial role in our company's success. Having a network of peers who had faced or were facing similar challenges was priceless. Later, I took it a step further by working with a one-on-one coach. Through this experience, I met Jeff, who introduced me to the concepts of culture, mission, vision, values, and team cohesion, concepts that transformed my leadership approach.

Through Jeff, I had the privilege of meeting Admiral John "Boomer" Stufflebeem, USN Retired. Boomer's extensive leadership experience at the highest levels of service to the United States provided me with an unparalleled education in real leadership. With Jeff and Boomer as mentors, I gained a deeper understanding of leadership principles that continue to shape my professional journey.

After three to four years of mentorship, Jeff and Boomer encouraged me to join them at the Professional Business Coaches Alliance (PBCA) and become a coach myself. Initially, I had no plans to pursue coaching full-time until I retired from my construction company. However, the timing aligned perfectly, and I launched my own construction peer group. Now, I have the privilege of giving back by passing on the invaluable knowledge I received from my mentors to others in the industry.

With over 25 years of construction experience, I am confident in my ability to help organizations achieve meaningful results. Through Construction Mastermind Peer Groups, one-on-one coaching, and tailored programs designed specifically for the construction industry, I am committed to helping businesses grow and succeed. If you're looking for guidance to elevate your business, don't hesitate to reach out. There's a program for you, and I'm here to help.

You can email me at: eric@freedomforgegroup.com

DEDICATION

This book is dedicated to my wife, Sara, and my two kids, Reid and Allie; to my family and friends, some of whom are my clients; and to the many wonderful business coaches and mentors I have been lucky enough to learn from over the years.

To my wife, I want to say thank you for always believing in me. Thank you for putting up with my crazy ideas, even if the timing always seems off. From starting a construction company with two young kids at home years ago to now, thank you for allowing me to chase my passion and for always being there through the long hours it takes to run a company.

To my friends, who've been there with an ear to listen and positive words of encouragement. Andrew D, Andrew J, Chris K, Dylan S, Ben H, Jordan L, Eric B, Jon T, and Troy M; thank you from the bottom of my heart for your support, your encouragement to do something I'm passionate about, and for helping me to grow my coaching and consulting firm. You guys have always believed in me; when I had low points in my career, you've always been there to pick me up and brush off the dust.

To my amazing coaches and mentors. George Hedley, thank you for accepting a young business owner into one of your peer groups. I thought I had it all figured out, just to realize that I really knew nothing at all! Had it not been for your peer group, I would not have understood the power of collective wisdom, and I would not have met so many other great business coaches, nor would I have started my own groups!

Jeff Rogers, thank you for taking a chance on me years ago as a client. You've guided me on a journey of transformation from a business owner to a coach. You've taught me about the power of effective communication, and I am deeply indebted to you for everything you've given me.

John "Boomer" Stufflebeam, where do I even start? You've been a pivotal part of my leadership development. You've helped me see things from the 30,000-foot view that most will never get the opportunity to see. From our awesome conversations about Detroit Lions Football, Jimmy Buffett, and Key West, thanks for believing in me, and I'm proud to call both you and Jeff my friends.

Thank you to Jim Petersen and the other great coaches at the PBCA for welcoming me and believing in me as a new coach, and for providing continuous training opportunities and support.

I also want to thank Craig Tobin for taking a chance on me years ago, when I was a young project manager at Pirc Tobin Construction. You've spent countless hours training and molding me to focus on the big picture, the people, the numbers, and not to sweat the small stuff!

And to all the others who've positively impacted my life, thank you from the bottom of my heart!

Section One

LEADING THE CHARGE

Chapter 1

IRON SHARPENS IRON

From Lone Operator to Leadership Collaborator

Just as iron sharpens iron, leaders are refined through the friction of honest feedback, shared experience, and accountability. No one becomes sharper in isolation. Early in my career, I thought leadership meant having all the answers, pushing harder, working longer, and carrying every burden myself. But over time, I discovered that real strength doesn't come from doing it alone; it comes from being willing to learn from others. Coaching and peer groups became the forge that shaped me, challenging my assumptions, expanding my perspective, and transforming how I led both people and business.

How Coaching and Peer Groups Helped Me Grow My Business

Running a construction business is no small feat. It demands balancing the technical side of the work, production schedules, safety, and client expectations, with the human side of leadership, communication, and decision-making. For years, I tried to shoulder it all on my own, convinced that asking for help was a sign of weakness.

But as the business grew, the weight of that mindset became impossible to carry.

It wasn't until I joined a peer group and began working with a business coach that things truly started to change. Those conversations opened my eyes to blind spots I didn't know I had. I learned to see challenges through the eyes of others who had walked the same path, business owners who understood the pressures, sacrifices, and tough calls that come with leadership. They didn't tell me what I wanted to hear; they told me what I needed to hear.

Through coaching and peer accountability, I became a better listener, decision-maker, and leader. I began to focus less on managing the day-to-day and more on building systems, empowering people, and aligning my company with a greater purpose. What started as an effort to grow my business became a journey to grow myself.

The Turning Point: Recognizing I Needed Help

When I started my construction business, I was confident in my technical skills and industry knowledge. But as the company expanded, I found myself overwhelmed by:

- ➢ Managing multiple crews and projects.
- ➢ Dealing with unpredictable cash flow and tight profit margins.
- ➢ Struggling to delegate effectively.
- ➢ Feeling isolated in decision-making.

The harder I worked, the more I felt like I was spinning my wheels. That's when I realized that being a great builder didn't automatically make me a great business leader. I needed help overcoming the challenges and growing my business sustainably.

How Business Coaching Transformed My Leadership

I decided to hire a business coach, and the experience was transformative. Here's how coaching helped me:

> **Clarifying My Vision and Goals**
>
> My coach helped me articulate a clear vision for my business, focusing on long-term success rather than short-term problem-solving. One of the first things we did was to create our Mission, Vision, and Values Statement. This allows us to openly share what our mission is and how we get there. I set specific, measurable goals for growth, profitability, and work–life balance. The goals also have to be scalable. Don't just say you want to do $50,000,000 in sales next year when you are only a $3,000,000 company right now. You can get there, but you need to have a plan.

> **Building Leadership Skills**
>
> Coaching helped me develop the skills to lead effectively, such as delegation, conflict resolution, and communication. These skills are not learned overnight, but they are earned with practice and

patience. I learned to empower my team and trust them to take ownership of their responsibilities, freeing me to focus on strategic decisions and sales.

➤ **Creating Systems and Processes**

My coach guided me in developing written systems and standard operating procedures (SOPs) to streamline operations and reduce chaos. We will talk more about Systems and SOPs later on in the book and how these are extremely important for organizations of any size. With these systems in place, my business became more efficient and scalable. We essentially had internal rules for the way we do things.

➤ **Improving Financial Management**

I learned how to analyze key financial metrics, set realistic budgets, and prioritize high-margin projects. I had to get off the hamster wheel of low-bid public work. My coaches taught me how to manage cash flow more effectively, which reduced stress and improved profitability. Consider the questions that matter: Is the markup on a small project the same as a large project? Which customers pay fast versus those who don't? Is there a gap in our schedule to fill? All those should play key roles when pricing out a project.

➤ **Shifting My Mindset**

Perhaps the most impactful change was in my mindset. I moved from reacting to challenges to proactively planning for success. In Rich Horwath's book *Strategic*, he says, "Are You Ready Fire Aim or are you Ready Aim Fire?" Shifting from reactive to proactive takes time, but it will pay dividends in the end. I began to view setbacks as opportunities to learn and grow, which made me more resilient as a leader. As issues arose, I began asking our staff what they thought they could do differently next time to prevent them from happening again.

➢ **The Power of Peer Groups**

In addition to business coaching, I joined a peer group of fellow construction business owners. This group provided a different but equally valuable form of support.

➢ **Shared Experiences and Insights**

Hearing how others navigated challenges similar to mine gave me fresh perspectives, practical ideas, and opportunities for growth. I learned new strategies for marketing, client relations, and project management from peers who had already tried and tested them. Peer groups are a sounding board; nothing will test an idea quite like talking it through with peers and getting honest feedback.

➢ **Accountability**

Peer groups provided built-in accountability. Sharing my goals and progress with the group motivated me to stay focused and follow through on commitments. No one wants to be the person in a room in the same place, or in some cases a worse place, than they were at the previous meeting. You not only get accountability from your peers but also from your peer group coach.

➢ **Networking Opportunities**
Connecting with other business owners opened doors to new partnerships, subcontractors, and clients. Some individuals in the group, even though they are from different states, were able to help one another out on projects and resources. The group became a trusted network I could rely on for advice, resources, and referrals. I remember one guy shared his corporate use of the company credit card policy with me. His attorney had just wrapped it up, and he said, "Here, use mine, just change what you need for company information, and make it work for you."

➢ **Support During Tough Times**
Running a business can be isolating, but my peer group offered a sense of community. They say it's lonely at the top. Having a community of leaders and knowing that they are right there with you is reassuring. During challenging periods, the group provided encouragement and practical solutions to help me stay on track. They provide collective wisdom to explore new growth opportunities or markets.

Key Lessons I Learned from Coaching and Peer Groups

➢ **You Can't Do it All Alone**
One of the biggest mistakes I made early on was thinking I had to have all the answers. Accepting

help from experts and peers made all the difference. I remember showing up to the first peer group and thinking I had it all figured out. I quickly learned I knew nothing, nothing compared to those who had been involved in the group for a while.

> **Investing in Yourself is Investing in Your Business**
The time and money I spent on coaching and peer groups paid off many times over. By becoming a better leader, I improved every aspect of my business.

I learned how to lead effectively; I learned what worked and what didn't, so I hopefully wouldn't make the same mistake one of my peers did.

When it comes to Return on Investment (ROI), 68% of individuals who hired coaches were able to recover their investment. Those who realized a financial gain from coaching can, on average, expect a return of 3.44 times the amount spent.

Among companies that could calculate their ROI, 86% said they at least recovered their initial investment. Nineteen percent indicated an ROI of 50 times the investment, and 28% saw an ROI of 10 to 49 times the investment. The median company return was 7 times the initial investment (ICF Global Coaching Client Study, International Coach Federation, in consultation with PricewaterhouseCoopers LLP and Association Resource Centre Inc., April 2009).

According to a study by the International Society for Performance Improvement, coaching produces a 221%

ROI. Moreover, 51% of companies with a strong coaching culture report higher revenue than their industry peer group (Human Capital Institute).

➢ **Focus on What You Can Control**
Both coaching and peer groups helped me stop wasting energy on things outside my control, and instead focus on strategies to improve my business.

➢ **Continuous Learning is Essential**
The construction industry is always evolving, and so are the challenges of running a business. Staying open to new ideas and approaches keeps you ahead of the curve.

➢ **Accountability Drives Results**
Whether it's a coach holding you accountable for your goals or a peer group expecting updates on your progress, having someone to answer to keeps you motivated and disciplined.

The Results: A Stronger, More Successful Business

Thanks to business coaching and peer group support, my construction company was in a much stronger position. Some of the tangible results include:

➢ **Increased Profitability:** By focusing on high-margin projects and improving cash flow management, we significantly boosted our bottom line.

➢ **Scalable Operations:** With systems and processes in place, we can take on larger projects without sacrificing quality or efficiency.

> **Improved Work–Life Balance:** Delegating more effectively and focusing on strategy allowed me to step back from the day-to-day grind, spend more time with my family, and focus on building the business.

> **Stronger Team:** My employees are more engaged and empowered, resulting in higher morale and lower turnover.

Advice for Other Construction Business Owners

If you're feeling stuck or overwhelmed, I strongly recommend seeking out a business coach or joining a peer group. Here are some tips to get started:

> **Find the Right Fit**
> Look for a coach or group with experience in the construction industry to ensure their advice is relevant to your challenges.

> **Be Open to Feedback**
> Growth requires honesty and a willingness to hear tough feedback. Approach coaching and peer discussions with an open mind. If you are not willing to fix what's broken, don't bother. Sometimes we, the business owners, are the problem. As Patrick Lencioni reminds us, real progress begins when leaders are willing to be vulnerable and own their part.

> **Commit to the Process**
> Coaching and peer groups aren't quick fixes. They require time, effort, and commitment, but the

rewards are worth it. All it takes is one little nugget of information to take back to your organization that can make a positive impact both financially and strategically. After all, you rely on the group and the group relies on you; if you don't commit, you may miss your nugget, or another member may miss the nugget you would have otherwise provided.

➢ **Take Action**

Insight is only valuable if you apply it. Use what you learn to make concrete changes in your business. Don't just say you are going to do it, actually do it. I find it best to implement changes sooner rather than later, otherwise they will always be on your to-do list. Put a plan in place, leverage the team you have at your organization, include them in the process to get their buy-in, and do it!

Conclusion

Business coaching and peer groups gave me the tools, insights, and confidence to transform my construction company. They helped me move from survival mode to growth mode, building a business I was proud of, and a team I could rely on.

If you're facing challenges in your business, remember this: you don't have to figure it all out on your own. Surround yourself with people who can guide and support you, and you'll be amazed at what you can achieve. However, the ultimate commitment lies on your shoulders; no one is going to do the work for you. Yet, once you start to transform your organization and you see those positive results, you will then know it was all worth it, and you are able to take action much quicker on other issues as they arise.

Leadership isn't about knowing everything; it's about knowing where to learn and whom to learn from. Coaches and peer groups sharpen your leadership edge, much like rebar strengthens concrete, unseen, but essential.

Leadership Builder

Ask yourself:

> ➤ Who are my trusted voices that tell me what I need to hear, not what I want to hear?
> ➤ How can I create "micro peer groups" within my company to promote shared learning?

Chapter 2

KNOW YOUR WHY

Purpose: The Anchor of Leadership

Purpose gives direction when the storm hits. In both construction and leadership, your "why" is the rebar that keeps your structure from collapsing under pressure.

Every organization, team, and individual operates with a purpose—an underlying reason for what they do. Yet, in the hustle of daily operations, this "why" can be forgotten and replaced by a focus on tasks, deadlines, and outputs. Understanding your "why" is essential for maintaining focus, motivation, and alignment. This chapter explores the importance of knowing your "why," how to uncover it, and how it serves as a foundation for personal and professional success.

What is Your "Why?"

Your "why" is your purpose, your driving force. It answers the fundamental question: why do we do what we do? It goes beyond profit, goals, or metrics; it's the core reason that inspires action and creates meaning. For individuals, it might be tied to personal values or life aspirations. For organizations, it reflects the impact they aim to have on the world, customers, or communities. It's their mission statement. Knowing your why serves as a compass: guiding decisions and behaviors. Without it, actions can feel aimless, and even success can seem hollow.

Why Knowing Your Why Matters

Identifying and embracing your why has transformative benefits for individuals, teams, and organizations:

> **Purpose Drives Motivation**
>
> When people understand the deeper reason behind their work, they find greater fulfillment and energy. Purpose connects daily tasks to a larger vision, turning mundane efforts into meaningful contributions.

> **Alignment Enhances Focus**
>
> A clear "why" helps filter out distractions and prioritize actions that align with core values and goals. It keeps individuals and teams moving in the same direction, even when facing challenges.

> **Resilience During Challenges**
>
> Purpose acts as a stabilizer during tough times. Knowing your why provides clarity and determination to navigate setbacks, adapt, and persevere. Some of the most successful leaders are highly resilient and won't let change stop them. They adapt to the current challenge and find alternative ways to overcome it.

> **Connection Builds Engagement**
>
> A shared purpose fosters stronger relationships. Teams and organizations that know their why create

cultures of trust, collaboration, and loyalty, which makes it easier to attract and retain talent.

➤ **Authenticity Inspires Others**

Leaders and organizations that operate from a place of purpose exude authenticity. Customers, partners, and employees are drawn to this clarity and passion, creating lasting connections. If you're the owner, this authenticity starts with you. It's your job to portray your passion to your team, and allow them to feel the same passion—ultimately and seamlessly portraying this to your customers and building a strong bond with those you serve.

How to Discover Your Why

Uncovering your why requires introspection, open communication, and a willingness to dig deeper. Here's how individuals and organizations can identify their purpose:

For Individuals:

➤ **Reflect on Your Values:** What principles guide your life? Consider what matters most to you: integrity, innovation, or making a difference. For me, it is servant leadership. Helping others is my passion. And to dig deeper: helping construction and trades companies along with business owners find their why—in order to grow both personally and professionally—is what drives me!

➤ **Examine Your Passions:** What excites you? What work makes you lose track of time, because it feels meaningful? While putting my thoughts to paper for this book, words just poured out. I'm pretty sure my wife thought I was nuts when I told her I was writing a book! I would attribute some of this inspiration to Dr. Tracey Jones and her book, *SPARK: Five Essentials to Ignite the Greatness Within*. I met Dr. Jones at a Professional Business Coaches Alliance (PBCA) conference in Dallas. She was a guest speaker and was leading the PBCA's Certified Professional Business Leader (CPBL) program. The CPBL program is designed to make business owners become business leaders. During Dr. Jones' segment, I was inspired by her wisdom, wit, and compassion for helping others and just like her book titled *Spark*, one was ignited in me!

➢ **Identify Impact:** Who or what do you want to influence positively? How do you want to make the world or your community better? In 2006, my Uncle Alan Zazza passed away unexpectedly. He was a successful business owner, wonderful husband to my Aunt Karen, and father to my two cousins Michelle and Holly. To me, besides being my uncle, he was a friend, mentor, and someone who was well respected in our local community here in Iowa. I remember at his funeral how the line for the wake or viewing was long and lasted until the funeral home closed that night. I believe we even had to keep it open longer, just to get everyone through to pay their respects.

Then as I grew older, I began to define what success is. To me, it wasn't money or power; rather, it was the impact that you left on others. So, for me, in this instance success was defined by the number of people who showed up to pay their respects on a cold January day in Iowa for such an amazing individual. They showed up to respect someone who had made an impact in their life.

> **Look Back at Milestones:** Reflect on your proudest achievements. What was fulfilling about them? What values or goals did they align with?
> **Ask Why, Repeatedly:** Dig deep by asking yourself why you do what you do, then ask why, again. This process uncovers layers of meaning.

How I came to my "Why"

After I sold my construction company, I was stuck in what I call the "Milk Bowl"—that fog of uncertainty or lost in the clouds. I had just come out of a 25-year career in the concrete construction industry and had to figure out what to do next. My first instinct was to immediately start another construction company, but somehow it didn't feel right. The summer before I sold my company, I was invited to join the PBCA. I got certified as a coach and after having been involved with coaching and business peer groups for 8 years, I decided to put together a peer group of my own. This was one of the most fulfilling things I'd ever done as a business owner. Now let's fast-forward to the "Milk Bowl" again: Just a few days in, I was no longer reporting to my office, and seeing employees daily; but I was reporting to my home office and was feeling scared, confused, anxious, and all the other emotions that go along with uncertainty. I remember having dinner with Michael Anderson, one of our amazing Master Coaches at the PBCA, and he asked me, "What is it that you really want to do? If there's one thing you could do and money isn't an issue, what would that be?" That was a loaded question, let me tell you! In the construction industry, I had always got a sense of accomplishment after completing a project. Yet with coaching, the projects are always evolving; being able to see results with clients and their organizations brought a new and higher sense of accomplishment to me. I believe Michael could sense that, as well as a couple of my other coaches: Jeff and Boomer. They could sense this passion too, which is what led to my invite into the PBCA. So, from these conversations, I decided to go all in on my coaching and consulting company—ultimately putting in the same effort that it would take to start another construction company. My passion for helping others is now something I get to do day in and day out. Building great teams and amazing leaders is my why. Although I can't say that someday I won't get back into the trades as a business owner or CEO for an organization, one thing is for certain: I will enjoy this journey and the path chosen for me either way!

I feel most comfortable in the world of construction, so the majority of my clients are from that industry. The question I always ask myself is: "How do I help as many people as I can?" Businesses, employees, and even friends. It's about building and growing the next generation of great leaders.

For Organizations:

➢ **Examine Your Origins:** Why was the organization founded? What problem is it trying to solve or what need it aims to fulfill?

➢ **Engage Stakeholders:** Involve employees, customers, and partners in discussions about the company's purpose. Their insights can help refine the why.

➢ **Define Your Impact:** What positive change do you want to create for your customers, community, or industry?

➢ **Clarify Your Core Values:** What principles guide your organization's decisions and behaviors?

➢ **Articulate a Vision:** Combine your purpose, values, and impact into a concise statement that resonates with all stakeholders.

Living Your Why

Knowing your why is only the first step; living it brings it to life. Here are the strategies for ensuring your purpose remains at the forefront:

➢ **Communicate it Clearly**

For individuals, share your why with those around you to build accountability and inspire others. For organizations, integrate your purpose into messaging, training, and decision-making.

➢ **Embed it in Culture**

Organizations should align policies, incentives, and behaviors with their why. Employees should feel and see the purpose reflected in their daily work environment. Admiral McRaven once said, "The culture of your organization starts with you."

➤ **Revisit and Reaffirm**

Periodically revisit your why to ensure it still resonates. Life circumstances or market conditions may evolve, but your core purpose should remain a constant source of motivation.

➤ **Lead by Example**

Leaders must embody their why to inspire others. Authenticity starts at the top, whether through decisions, actions, or communication.

➤ **Celebrate Purpose-Driven Wins**

Recognize achievements that align with your why. Celebrating these moments reinforces the importance of staying connected to your purpose.

Conclusion: The Power of Why

Knowing your why is more than a motivational exercise; it's the foundation of sustained success and fulfillment. Whether you're an individual seeking personal growth or an organization striving to make an impact, your why provides direction, meaning, and resilience. Take time to uncover your purpose and let it guide your decisions, inspire your actions, and shape your legacy. When you know your why, you don't just do the work, you do it with intention, passion, and a clear sense of direction.

When your people understand the "why," they find meaning beyond the paycheck. Leaders who communicate purpose build loyalty and clarity—and culture that lasts.

Leadership Builder

Ask yourself:

- ➢ What story best explains *my* why?
- ➢ How often do I remind my team of the bigger purpose behind our work?

Chapter 3

THE POWER TRAP

Position isn't Leadership

Authority without influence fails. Fear can push productivity for a season, but it never produces loyalty. Respect lasts longer than authority.

Leadership in construction is a dynamic, multifaceted role that demands far more than a title or position. Many leaders fall into the *power trap*, believing authority alone can move people. But leading by position and power, relying solely on rank to command compliance, often breeds resentment, damages morale, and weakens results. True leadership isn't about control; it's about connection.

The relationship between a leader and their team should be built on trust, curiosity, and collaboration. When guidance replaces orders and respect replaces fear, people think for themselves, speak up, and take ownership. In an industry where every decision can impact safety, efficiency, and profitability, empowering people to think critically isn't a luxury; it's essential.

This chapter explores the pitfalls of authoritarian leadership and reveals why influence-based leadership creates stronger, safer, and more successful construction teams.

What Does Leading by Position and Power Look Like?

Leading by position and power means deriving authority primarily from one's title rather than from competence, credibility, or character. It's the "do it because I said so" approach; leadership by command, not collaboration.

This mindset often shows up as top–down orders with little room for discussion, micromanagement that strangles initiative, and fear-based compliance where employees follow instructions only to avoid reprimand. In this environment, people stop thinking critically. If a worker notices something built incorrectly, they might stay silent rather than risk being yelled at. The cost of fear-based leadership isn't just morale; it's mistakes, rework, and missed opportunities for improvement.

Rigid adherence to hierarchy discourages creativity, innovation, and ownership. While such a style might achieve short-term results, it creates long-term damage that undermines trust and team cohesion.

The Consequences of Power-Driven Leadership

When authority replaces authenticity, the fallout is predictable: morale drops, turnover rises, and innovation stalls. Employees who feel undervalued disengage. Without recognition or autonomy, they simply go through the motions. Over time, this creates a culture of minimal effort, where people do just enough to avoid conflict.

High turnover becomes the norm, as capable workers leave in search of respect and autonomy. Constant hiring and retraining drive costs up while slowing progress. Creativity disappears because no one feels safe sharing ideas that might challenge the status quo. Micromanagement breeds inefficiency, bottlenecks, and frustration, while poor communication leads to costly misunderstandings.

In these environments, trust is eroded. Teams operate in silos, and resistance to change becomes ingrained. The company might look stable on paper, but underneath, the foundation is cracked.

Why You Should Avoid Leading by Position and Power

Leadership is earned, not given. Titles may command initial respect, but sustained respect comes from integrity, consistency, and competence.

In construction, an industry that demands adaptability, rigid, power-based leadership becomes a liability. The best foremen, superintendents, and owners are those who listen, adjust, and empower. When teams are encouraged to collaborate and problem-solve, they respond faster to challenges and take greater pride in their work.

Reputation also matters. A leader known for arrogance or control may find that the best employees leave and the best clients stop calling. Conversely, leaders who empower others build organizations that outlast them. When trust replaces fear, growth becomes scalable; the business no longer depends on one person's authority, but on shared accountability and vision.

Escaping the Power Trap

Escaping the power trap begins with a shift in mindset: leadership is not about control, it's about connection. The moment a leader realizes that authority doesn't equal influence, everything changes. Progress happens when we replace fear with trust, compliance with commitment, and command with collaboration.

To move from managing by position to leading by purpose, focus should be on influence and not on intimidation. Build credibility through integrity, empathy, and competence. Foster collaboration by inviting ideas from every level of the organization. Empower employees to make decisions, providing them with the tools, training, and trust they need to succeed.

Practice servant leadership; serve your people so they can serve the mission. Communicate with honesty and transparency, especially during change. Recognize effort and celebrate achievement. When people feel seen and valued, they give their best.

True leadership doesn't demand loyalty; it earns it.

A Lesson from the Field

A mid-sized construction company once operated under a rigid, top–down structure. Every decision had to pass through the management. Employees followed orders, but rarely spoke up. Over time, morale dropped, innovation stopped, and turnover skyrocketed. Projects ran late, rework increased, and the company's reputation suffered.

When new leadership took over, they decided to change course. Instead of dictating every move, they began involving foremen and crew leaders in their planning meetings. Ideas from the field were welcomed and often implemented. Accountability grew naturally because people now had a voice in the process.

Within months, the results were undeniable: productivity improved, safety scores rose, and client satisfaction rebounded. The company hadn't just fixed its process; it had rebuilt its culture.

Conclusion

Leading by position and power may yield short-term compliance, but at the cost of employee morale, innovation, and organizational growth. True leadership is about building trust, fostering collaboration, and empowering employees to achieve their full potential. You, the leader, need to inspire them! By moving away from authoritarian practices and embracing influence-based leadership, construction leaders can create a resilient, dynamic, and thriving organization equipped to meet the challenges of a complex industry.

Construction crews don't follow titles, they follow trust. The moment people trust that you care more about them than your position, they'll run through walls for you.

Leadership Builder

Ask yourself:

> ➢ Where am I relying on authority instead of trust?
> ➢ What daily action can rebuild respect and influence?

Chapter 4

INFLUENCE OVER AUTHORITY

Turning Control into Confidence

Empowerment is the handoff between good leaders and great ones. When you release control, you grow capacity.

Effective leadership isn't about issuing commands or controlling every decision; it's about inspiring, influencing, and empowering employees to take ownership of their roles and contribute to the organization's success. In the construction industry, where teamwork, safety, and efficiency are paramount, leaders who lead by influence rather than authority create stronger teams and better outcomes. This chapter explores the principles of leadership by influence, the importance of empowering employees, and actionable strategies for fostering a culture of collaboration and trust.

The Core of Leadership by Influence

Leadership by influence involves guiding and motivating others through respect, trust, and shared purpose rather than hierarchical authority. Key traits of an influential leader include:

> **Authenticity:** Being genuine and consistent in actions and words builds trust and respect.

- ➢ **Emotional Intelligence (EQ):** Understanding and managing emotions, both your own and others', is critical to fostering strong relationships.
- ➢ **Vision:** Clearly articulating a compelling vision inspires others to work toward shared goals.
- ➢ **Empathy:** Demonstrating care and understanding for employees' perspectives and challenges enhances loyalty and engagement.
- ➢ **Credibility:** Leaders who model excellence and accountability gain the respect needed to influence effectively.

Why Empowerment Matters in Construction

Empowering employees involves giving them the tools, autonomy, and confidence to perform their roles effectively. In construction, where projects often depend on split-second decisions and on-the-ground problem-solving, empowerment is essential for:

- ➢ **Faster Decision-Making:** Empowered employees can address issues directly without waiting for managerial approval.
- ➢ **Improved Morale and Engagement:** Employees who feel trusted and valued are more motivated and committed to their work.
- ➢ **Innovation:** When employees are encouraged to think independently, they are more likely to suggest creative solutions.

➢ **Safety and Compliance:** Empowering employees to prioritize safety ensures adherence to standards and reduces workplace incidents.

➢ **Reduced Turnover:** Empowered teams are more likely to remain loyal to the organization, reducing the costs and disruption of high turnover rates.

Strategies for Leading by Influence

➢ **Lead by Example**

Demonstrate the values and behaviors you expect from your team, whether it's punctuality, work ethic, or respect for others. Show accountability by owning your mistakes and learning from them.

➢ **Build Trust**

Be transparent about decisions, challenges, and expectations. Follow through on commitments to show reliability and integrity.

➢ **Communicate Effectively**

Practice active listening to understand employees' concerns and ideas. Use clear, concise language to ensure everyone understands goals and expectations.

➢ **Foster Collaboration**

Encourage teamwork by creating opportunities for employees to share ideas and solve problems collectively.

Recognize and reward team achievements to reinforce collaboration.

➤ **Adapt Your Leadership Style**

Different situations and individuals require different approaches. Adapt your style to meet the unique needs of your team and project. Balance directive leadership with supportive coaching to build confidence and autonomy.

Empowering Employees in Practice

➤ **Provide Clear Expectations**

Define roles, responsibilities, and project goals to give employees a clear understanding of what is expected of them.

➤ **Offer Autonomy**

Avoid micromanaging and trust employees to make decisions within their scope of work. Encourage employees to take ownership of their tasks and problem-solving.

➤ **Invest in Development**

Provide ongoing training and development opportunities to enhance skills and career growth. Offer mentorship programs to guide less experienced employees.

➤ **Encourage Feedback and Innovation**

Create a culture where employees feel comfortable sharing ideas and concerns.

Act on employee feedback to show their voices matter.

➤ **Recognize and Reward Success**

Celebrate individual and team achievements to reinforce positive behaviors and outcomes.

Use both monetary and non-monetary recognition to show appreciation.

➢ **Equip Employees for Success**

Ensure employees have the tools, resources, and support they need to perform their roles effectively. Provide clear and accessible SOPs to guide their work.

Example: Influential Leadership in Action

A construction project manager noticed recurring delays due to communication breakdowns between on-site teams and management. Instead of imposing strict rules, the manager: Held team meetings to understand employees' concerns and gather feedback. Empowered team leads to make real-time decisions on-site. Provided training on communication tools to improve coordination. Recognized team members who demonstrated initiative and problem-solving. As a result, team morale improved, communication barriers were reduced, and the project was completed ahead of schedule. This example highlights how leadership by influence and empowerment can transform challenges into opportunities.

The Long-Term Impact of Leadership by Influence

Within my organization, I had a project assistant named Jodi. When she started, she was brand new to the construction industry, but eager to learn. Early on, she would stop by my office constantly with questions, and to be honest, it drove me nuts. I realized, though, that the problem wasn't her curiosity; it was my approach. Instead of giving her the answers, I started asking *her* questions: guiding her to think through the situation and find solutions on her own. Over time, Jodi grew from seeking direction to providing it. She became one heck of an employee, a capable Project Manager, and a respected professional in the industry.

Stronger Teams

Employees who feel valued and empowered are more likely to collaborate effectively and support one another. A few of the results are:

> **Increased Productivity:** Motivated employees take pride in their work, leading to higher quality and efficiency.

> **Resilient Culture:** A culture of trust and empowerment helps organizations adapt to change and overcome challenges.

> **Sustainable Growth:** Leaders who inspire and empower build a foundation for long-term organizational success.

Conclusion

Leadership by influence and the empowerment of employees are essential for thriving in the fast-paced, and demanding, construction industry. By fostering trust, collaboration, and autonomy, leaders can inspire their teams to achieve excellence, even in the face of challenges. Have you ever had that emerging leader in your organization always calling you for answers? What is your response? Do you answer the phone and tell them the answers they are looking for? Or do you avoid answering the phone, only to call back 30 minutes later to see that they have already resolved the issue—and to an extent that satisfies you? True leadership is not about controlling outcomes, but enabling people to reach their full potential; turning every project into a testament to the power of empowered individuals working toward a common vision. By allowing the employee to make time-sensitive decisions, you are building the confidence they need to become an amazing leader—and one of the unintended outcomes is you will receive less and less of those phone calls. At that point, it's up to you to check in and reassure the employees that the choices they are making are on point and you are impressed with their problem-solving abilities.

The best foremen and superintendents teach their crews how to think, not just what to do. Influence happens when your people make the right call, even when you're not there.

Leadership Builder

Ask yourself:

> ➤ Who on my team needs permission to lead?
> ➤ How can I practice "controlled delegation" to build confidence and accountability?

Chapter 5

EFFECTIVE COMMUNICATION

Meeting People Where They Are— The Leadership Multiplier

Communication is the bridge between intention and action. Leadership dies when that bridge collapses.

Effective communication is the foundation for building relationships, resolving conflict, and achieving shared goals. Yet one of the most overlooked aspects of communication is meeting people where they are—emotionally, intellectually, and situationally. Doing so requires empathy, adaptability, and a genuine commitment to understanding others' perspectives.

A powerful tool I use with organizations is an assessment called **Extended DISC**. It helps leaders and teams understand natural behavioral styles, so they can meet others where they are, instead of expecting everyone to meet them where *they* are. In this chapter, we'll explore practical ways to connect with people in ways that foster mutual respect, understanding, and collaboration.

Understanding "Where They Are"

Meeting people where they are begins with awareness. Every conversation carries emotional, intellectual, and situational factors that shape how messages are received. Ask yourself: *What emotional state is this person in?* Are they stressed, excited, or frustrated? Emotions drive perception. Consider their level of knowledge: how much do they already understand? Overloading someone with detail can be as ineffective as oversimplifying. Notice their communication style: are they direct or reflective, analytical or relational? Finally, recognize their current priorities. Addressing what matters most to them in the moment shows respect and builds trust.

When leaders take time to notice these dynamics, they can adjust their approach to create conversations that are both productive and supportive.

Active Listening

Active listening is the cornerstone of meaningful communication. Stephen Covey called it "Seeking first to understand, then to be understood." It's more than hearing words. It's being fully present. Maintain eye contact, remove distractions, and show attentiveness through body language. Ask clarifying questions to ensure you truly grasp what's being said: *"When you say you're overwhelmed, do you mean with deadlines or the overall workload?"* Reflect back what you've heard, *"It sounds like you're concerned about the project timeline."*

Perhaps, most importantly, free your mind from rehearsing your next response while the other person is talking. Listen to understand, not to reply. When people feel heard, they feel valued, and that validation builds lasting trust.

Empathy Over Ego

Empathy is the ability to step into another person's shoes and see the world through their lens. Too often, leaders focus on their own feelings or the point they want to make instead of truly grasping another person's experience. Empathy begins with acknowledging emotions without judgment: *"I can see why that situation would be frustrating."* Avoid assumptions; ask for clarification before drawing conclusions. When you respond, frame your words with care. If someone is upset, lead with reassurance before offering solutions.

A coach once told me, "Kiss first, kick second," praise before problem. When you recognize effort or emotion first, the feedback that follows is easier to accept and more likely to create change.

Adapting Your Communication Style

Not everyone communicates the same way, and great leaders recognize that their job isn't to change others but to adapt to them. Some people are analytical and want data; others are relational and respond to stories or emotion. Pay attention to the tone, pace, and body language to identify a person's preferred style, then mirror it appropriately.

Energy level matters, too. On a scale of one to ten, if someone is operating at a calm four, charging in at an eight will feel overwhelming. Bring yourself closer to their energy level to create connection rather than resistance.

Finally, choose the right medium. Some conversations require face-to-face dialogue, while others can be handled over email or text. Adaptability shows respect for how others process information and demonstrates emotional intelligence in action.

Focusing on Common Ground

People are far more receptive when they sense shared purpose. Start conversations by emphasizing what you both want to achieve. In the field, that might sound like, *"We both want this project to succeed, let's figure out the best way forward."* In personal relationships, it might be, *"I know time together matters to you, and I want that too. Let's find a balance."*

Finding common ground diffuses defensiveness and opens the door to cooperation. Agreement on values or goals provides a foundation for addressing differences productively.

Simplifying Without Patronizing

Great communicators make complex ideas simple, without making others feel small. Use examples that connect to the listener's world: a construction foreman understands "pouring the foundation" better than "establishing core processes." Break information into manageable pieces and check for understanding along the way: *"Does that make sense so far?"* Simplicity builds clarity, and clarity builds confidence.

Being Patient and Present

Meeting people where they are often takes patience. Rushing a conversation or forcing agreement creates resistance. Give others time to process, and let silence do the heavy lifting when needed. Stay mentally present rather than thinking ahead to your next point or multitasking. Remember that not every conversation will end in resolution; some will simply move the relationship forward one step at a time. Patience communicates respect for the other person's pace and priorities.

The Benefits of Meeting People Where They Are

When you intentionally adapt your communication to the person and situation, everything improves. Relationships grow stronger because people feel heard and valued. Outcomes improve as collaboration replaces confusion. Conflicts diminish because empathy de-escalates tension before it turns toxic. And your influence increases; people are more likely to follow a leader who takes the time to understand them.

Practical Examples

Consider a project manager who notices a normally outspoken crew member has grown quiet in meetings. Instead of calling them out publicly, the manager checks in privately, listens, and learns the employee is overwhelmed. A simple adjustment to workload restores engagement.

At home, a parent who wants their teenager to open up about school struggles doesn't lecture, they share their own story of frustration and failure, creating safety and trust.

Or imagine a ready-mix client angry about a delayed delivery. The representative listens fully, acknowledges the frustration, and outlines a plan to make it right. By listening first and solving second, the rep turns conflict into partnership.

In each case, communication succeeds because the leader met the other person where they were.

Conclusion

Meeting people where they are isn't about softening your message, it's about delivering it in a way that resonates. By practicing active listening, empathy, and adaptability, you transform communication from a transaction into a connection.

In my own practice, I use assessments such as **DISC**, **EQ 2.0**, and **AQai** to help leaders understand their teams more deeply, how they prefer to communicate, what motivates them, and where they feel valued or unseen. These insights become a roadmap for improving communication on both sides of the conversation.

Great leaders learn to read the room, match their tone to the moment, and listen longer than they talk. On the jobsite, that can be the difference between misunderstanding and motivation.

Leadership Builder

Ask yourself:

> ➤ Who on my team do I struggle to *read*, and why?
> ➤ How can I slow down, listen longer, and lead with understanding before I instruct?

Chapter 6

THE LEADERSHIP CYCLE

Refine the process, reinforce the standard, repeat the success

Leadership isn't a straight line; it's a continuous cycle: **Lead, Train, Evaluate, Adjust, and Repeat**. Skip any step, and the system breaks. In construction, where precision, safety, and efficiency are non-negotiable, training isn't a one-time event; it's the backbone of long-term success. True leaders understand that every interaction is an opportunity to teach, refine, and reinforce standards. Whether onboarding a new hire or developing a seasoned foreman, consistent training and evaluation keep crews aligned, confident, and capable. Great leaders don't just build projects, they build people—one cycle at a time.

The Role of Training in Construction

Training in construction reaches far beyond teaching technical skills. It shapes safety culture, sharpens project management, and strengthens leadership. Because construction is one of the most hazardous industries, comprehensive training saves lives and ensures compliance. It also drives efficiency and quality: a well-trained crew finishes faster with fewer errors and with pride in their work.

Training fuels adaptability too. As equipment, materials, and technology evolve, learning keeps companies competitive. Perhaps most importantly, training demonstrates that people are valued. When employees see their employer investing in their growth, morale rises, loyalty deepens, and turnover falls. Training isn't a cost; it's a signal of trust and belief in a person's potential.

Training for New Hires

The first few weeks on a jobsite shape how new employees see themselves and the company. A structured onboarding process accelerates confidence, competence, and connection. It begins with safety, the first and most important lesson. New hires should leave day one understanding the company's safety protocols, emergency procedures, and expectations for personal responsibility.

From there, leaders teach role-specific skills, combining classroom instruction with hands-on practice. Whether learning to operate a skid steer or read blueprints, new employees need guided repetition until proficiency becomes habit. Introducing them to company culture is equally important. Early conversations about values, teamwork, and communication standards set expectations that will last a career.

When onboarding is intentional, the results are powerful: faster productivity, fewer injuries, and higher confidence. Early investment also instills a growth mindset, teaching new hires that learning never stops. In turn, they become more adaptable, motivated, and loyal to the team that believed in them from day one.

One of my good friends, **Andrew Jackson**, owner of **TCE Construction** in Greeley, Colorado, built an outstanding onboarding program that completely transformed how his company develops people. Early in 2025, as he prepared to bring on a few new team members for upcoming projects, Andrew mentioned the plan during a crew meeting. Without hesitation, several of his employees spoke up: *"Can we onboard them the same way we did last time?"*

That simple request said everything. The team recognized the value of the process because they had lived it. The onboarding program blended hands-on training, one-on-one mentoring, and a clear path to success. The results spoke for themselves; those new hires quickly became some of the most productive and engaged employees in the company.

Andrew's approach is proof that **when you invest the time to train and mentor intentionally, you don't just fill positions, you build people**. And that investment pays dividends long after the job is done. We'll explore this idea further in the next chapter, where we look at how intentional mentoring and leadership development can turn good employees into great leaders.

Training for Mid-Level Leaders

As employees grow, so must their training. Mid-level leaders, foremen, crew leads, and estimators sit at the heart of execution. Their development determines whether strategy becomes reality.

At this stage, training focuses on advanced technical mastery and leadership readiness. Workers learn specialized tools, software, and evolving construction methods. But skill alone isn't enough; they also learn to manage people. Through leadership development sessions, they study communication, conflict resolution, and behavioral tools such as **DISC**, which help them understand and motivate different personalities.

They're introduced to project-management principles, scheduling, budgeting, resource allocation—all designed to give them ownership beyond the jobsite. As a result, they lead with greater confidence, manage time more effectively, and build stronger crews. When a foreman understands both the blueprint and the people behind it, projects run smoother and morale runs higher. Growth at this level also reduces turnover: people rarely leave a company when they see a path to advancement.

Training for Senior Management

Even the most experienced leaders must keep learning. Project managers, executives, and company owners face complex challenges, market shifts, regulations, new technology, and workforce development. The phrase "you don't know what you don't know" applies here more than anywhere.

Training for senior leaders centers on strategic leadership and vision. They learn how to make high-stakes decisions, balance risk, and plan for long-term sustainability. They stay current with emerging technologies such as Building Information Modeling (BIM), drones, and data analytics, integrating innovation into daily operations. They also refresh their understanding of safety and labor regulations, ensuring compliance and protecting the company's reputation.

Equally vital are soft skills, emotional intelligence, negotiation, and communication. These determine how effectively leaders inspire others, navigate conflict, and model the culture they expect from their teams. A senior leader who invests in personal growth sets the tone for everyone below them. In my experience, the years we spent the *most* money on leadership development were also our *most* profitable years.

The Importance of Continuous Evaluation

Training without evaluation is like pouring concrete without checking the forms: it won't hold. Every training program should include measurable feedback loops to ensure lessons translate to performance. Leaders can track productivity, safety, and quality metrics to gauge progress. Employee feedback reveals whether sessions felt relevant and engaging, while direct observation shows how well new skills appear in the field.

Follow-up sessions close the loop, addressing gaps or reinforcing key points. This accountability ensures that training remains a living system rather than a one-time event. When done consistently, evaluation not only proves return on investment but also builds a culture of reflection;

one where everyone, from apprentice to executive, asks: *How can we do this better next time?*

Conclusion: Lead, Train, Evaluate—Repeat

In the construction industry, where precision, safety, and teamwork are critical, training is not a luxury, it's a necessity. From equipping new hires with the fundamentals to preparing senior managers for strategic challenges, training ensures that every member of the team contributes to the company's success. By committing to lead, train, and evaluate effectively, organizations can create a culture of continuous improvement and adaptability. This not only enhances project outcomes but also fosters a more engaged and capable workforce. Invest in your people, and they will build your company's future, literally and figuratively.

Every jobsite is a classroom. When leaders teach, coach, and review consistently, they build habits that outlast them. The best construction companies aren't built on projects; they're built on people who are constantly learning.

Leadership Builder

Ask yourself:

> ➤ How often do I give feedback that develops rather than disciplines?
> ➤ What am I doing to grow my replacement?

Chapter 7

INVEST IN YOUR PEOPLE

The Return on Leadership Investment

A paycheck keeps people working. Purpose, growth, and gratitude keep them loyal.

In the construction industry where teamwork, trust, and skill development determine success, the most valuable asset any company has is its people. Leaders who intentionally invest in their workforce through training, development, recognition, and support build a culture where employees give their best because they feel their best. Investing in your people isn't just a feel-good idea, it's a business strategy that pays measurable dividends in loyalty, performance, and profitability.

The Business Case for Investing in People

When leaders pour into their teams, the return is undeniable. Companies that invest in employees see higher productivity, stronger retention, and greater innovation.

Employees who feel supported and valued perform at a higher level. A construction company that regularly updates its crews on new equipment or installation methods not only reduces downtime but also increases efficiency and quality. They don't just work harder, they work smarter.

Retention improves as well. When people see a future for themselves within an organization, they stop looking elsewhere. Considering that replacing a single employee can cost $10,000 or more, reducing turnover directly protects profit margins.

Word also travels fast in construction. Companies known for taking care of their people attract top talent and earn trust from clients who can sense the strength of the culture behind the work. And when employees are encouraged to learn and share new ideas, innovation follows. If you stifle creativity, you eventually stall growth. When you fuel it, you multiply it.

Ways to Invest in Your People

Training and Development

Few investments yield a greater return than helping employees grow their skills. They provide opportunities for certifications, on-the-job learning, and leadership development; send your foremen to workshops.

Support your operators in earning Occupational Safety and Health Administration (OSHA) or American Concrete Institute (ACI) credentials.

When I went through my local Associated General Contractors (AGC) chapter's *Leadership Academy* years ago, I was part of the eighth graduating class. It was uncomfortable at first—new faces, new challenges—but that experience stretched me as a leader and built lifelong industry connections. Training does more than developing competence; it develops confidence.

Career Growth Opportunities

Show employees they have a path forward. Cross-training allows people to explore new roles and find where they truly excel. One ready-mix driver I worked with learned to operate a concrete pump truck and quickly realized he loved it. He was happier, more productive, and became a leader others wanted to follow. Growth creates engagement.

Recognition and Reward

Acknowledging hard work is simple, but it's powerful. A few sincere words during a crew meeting, a public shout-out on social media, or a small bonus after a tough project can mean more than you realize. People don't just want a paycheck, they want to know they matter.

Supporting Work–Life Balance

Balanced employees are productive employees. Offer flexibility when possible and encourage time off after long stretches in the field. One of my mentors, Admiral John "Boomer" Stufflebeem, always said, *"Time off is an investment in future productivity."* It's true; rested people make better decisions, work safer, and lead stronger.

Creating a Positive Work Environment

A culture of respect and safety builds trust. Encourage open communication and let your people know mistakes are opportunities to learn, not weapons to punish.

I worked with a company once where employees stopped reporting equipment damage because management reacted harshly to every incident. The result was downtime, mistrust, and fear. If leadership had just shifted their mindset from punishment to problem-solving, the culture would've changed. Equipment would've gotten repaired faster, morale would've improved, and productivity would've followed.

When employees feel safe to speak up, everyone wins.

The Ripple Effect

When you invest in your people, the impact ripples far beyond the individual. Loyal employees stay through challenges. They protect your reputation and your brand. Teams collaborate more effectively because trust replaces competition.

And your company becomes a magnet for top talent. Skilled tradespeople talk. When word spreads that your organization funds apprenticeships, invests in certifications, and genuinely cares about growth, the best workers will find their way to your door.

Overcoming Barriers

Some leaders hesitate to invest in their people because of cost, time, or resistance to change. But those barriers are easier to overcome than you might think.

> ➢ **Budget constraints** shouldn't stop you. Start small with mentorship, toolbox talks, or in-house training. As you track results, you'll see the return justify further investment.

> **Resistance to change** fades when people are part of the process. Let key employees help design new systems or training programs. Their buy-in determines success.

> **Time constraints** can be managed by integrating learning into daily routines, quick tailgate sessions, brief debriefs after shifts, or scheduling workshops during slower months. Continuous improvement doesn't require large blocks of time; it requires consistent intention.

Measuring the Impact

Leadership is measurable. Track employee satisfaction through surveys, monitor turnover before and after implementing programs, and compare productivity or safety metrics over time. Even simple feedback forms can reveal what's working and what's not.

I've found that the years companies spend the most on training and leadership are often the years they see the greatest profitability. When you invest in people, they invest back in productivity, innovation, and culture.

Real-World Examples

A mid-sized construction firm once committed to mandatory safety training for every employee, from laborers to project managers. Within a year, recordable incidents dropped by 40%. Insurance costs fell, morale rose, and the company's reputation for safety attracted new business.

Another contractor built a *Career Pathways* program to

help laborers move into equipment-operator or supervisory roles. Within three years, turnover decreased by 30%, and efficiency climbed across multiple divisions. Growth wasn't just happening, it was compounding.

Building Trust Through Investment

Investing in employees goes far beyond financial rewards. It's about showing genuine care for their growth and well-being. When people know their leaders are committed to their success, not just the company's bottom line, they respond with loyalty, pride, and effort. Trust isn't built through policy; it's built through presence, consistency, and follow-through.

The Long-Term Return

A skilled, loyal workforce is the most reliable foundation a construction company can build on. It sustains growth through good markets and bad, strengthens client relationships through quality and consistency, and cultivates a culture of pride and ownership.

Employees who feel valued deliver higher-quality work, which builds client trust and repeat business. A company's reputation for care and integrity starts on the inside and radiates outward. When you take care of your people, they take care of your customers, and your brand.

Conclusion

In construction, every project depends on the expertise, dedication, and teamwork of your people. Investing in them isn't optional; it's essential. Provide opportunities for growth. Recognize effort. Create an environment where learning and loyalty thrive.

Every dollar and every hour you spend developing your team pays dividends in safety, productivity, and morale. People don't leave companies; they leave leaders who stopped investing in them.

The principle is simple but powerful: **take care of your people, and they'll take care of your company**. When you invest in your workforce, you're not just building careers, you're building a legacy.

Leadership Builder

Ask yourself:

> ➢ Where am I currently investing in my people?
> ➢ What small recognition could make a big impact this week?

Chapter 8

FROM LABORER TO LEADER: FORGED BY WORK

Leadership Forged in the Field

Leadership isn't handed out like a hard hat—it's earned through grit, humility, and service. Every concrete pour, every early morning, every mistake shaped who we became as leaders.

The First Pour

I remember my first day like it was yesterday: back in 1999, shovel in hand, sweat on my back, and not a clue where this path would lead. I wasn't thinking about leadership, strategy, or building a business. I was just trying to survive the day as the new guy on a concrete crew.

It was spring. My uncle's hotel and convention center was between events, so work had slowed down. My brother called one afternoon and said, *"We're short-handed, come help us."* That one phone call changed my life.

Every great leader starts somewhere. Usually, it's not behind a desk, it's in the dirt, shoulder to shoulder with the people doing the work.

The Foundation of Leadership

Starting out as a laborer in 1999, construction looked a lot different than it does today. The work was hard, the culture was rough, and at the end of the day you wore more dirt than dignity. Many guys would hit the bar, blow off steam, and do it all again the next morning.

But I always believed it didn't have to be that way. I wanted to prove that this industry, *our* industry, was about more than hard labor. It could be a career, a craft, and a calling.

That's where leadership begins: by showing up, staying late, asking questions, and taking pride in the work. Those moments—pouring concrete in the heat, laying curb in the dark, finishing that last sidewalk square—became my foundation.

A *job* is something you do for a paycheck. A *career* is something you build with passion. A job ends when the whistle blows. A career lives in the satisfaction of seeing something solid that you helped create.

The Mindset Shift

As I grew from laborer to foreman, I realized leadership wasn't about knowing it all; it was about knowing your people.

Get to know them, learn their stories, their hobbies, their families, their struggles. That personal connection builds trust and loyalty, and trust is the concrete that holds any team together.

I once had a boss who could manage a project but couldn't manage people. He ruled with intimidation, not influence.

It worked for a while, but it also burned people out. Years later, I ran into him at a conference. He was calmer, wiser. Maybe he'd learned what I had to learn the hard way: that leadership without empathy is just authority in disguise.

When I later became a project manager for a civil earthwork and utility company, I met a mentor named Craig. He didn't just teach me construction; he taught me ownership.

During bid reviews, Craig asked so many questions I could barely keep up. So, I started preparing answers *before* he asked. I learned to think ahead, to anticipate problems, to take responsibility for the results.

That's when it clicked: leadership means *owning the outcome*, even when it's uncomfortable.

Leaders don't provide every answer, they develop others who can. That's how you build buy-in, confidence, and future leaders.

Learning to Lead Yourself

One of my biggest lessons came through self-awareness. I've always been high-energy, vibrating at a ten on a scale of one to ten. That intensity served me well on the job, but not always with people.

When I took my first **DISC** assessment, it was eye-opening. I realized communication isn't one-size-fits-all. I had to learn to bring my energy down to a seven, instead of a ten, to meet people where they were. That small adjustment changed everything.

It led me deeper into leadership, servant leadership, and emotional intelligence. I started reading, attending peer groups, and seeking mentors. The more I learned, the more I saw what true leadership is:

> ➤ Leadership isn't about position, it's about permission.
> ➤ Permission earned through trust, consistency, and genuine care.

Leadership is Forged, Not Given

That belief eventually became the foundation of my coaching and consulting firm, Freedom Forge Group. Leadership, like metal, is formed under heat and pressure. It's not handed to you, it's hammered out through experience, mistakes, and perseverance.

I've seen many people who can run a jobsite, but can't lead a team. And I've seen laborers—quiet, overlooked, and underestimated—grow into some of the strongest leaders I've ever known.

One of those people is **Abel**.

Abel's Story: A Modern Leader in the Making

When Abel joined our team, he was quiet and focused. He didn't complain about the weather, the hours, or the workload. He showed up early, stayed late, and always asked thoughtful questions.

What set Abel apart wasn't just work ethic, it was humility. When something went wrong, he owned it. When things went right, he shared the credit. Over time, his crew started following him not because they had to, but because they *wanted* to.

That's leadership.

Today, Abel is one of the most respected people I've worked with. He leads with his head, heart, and hands. He's proof that leadership isn't found in a title, it's earned through trust and consistency.

Watching Abel grow reminds me why I do what I do. We didn't just build driveways or parking lots, we built *leaders*. And that's how culture is formed: one pour, one person, one lesson at a time.

Blueprint: From Laborer to Leader

There's no shortcut. No secret formula. But every leader I've met follows a familiar pattern.

1. **Show Up Ready**–Reliability is rare. Be the person others can count on every single day.
2. **Be Coachable**–Great leaders never stop learning. Feedback isn't failure, it's fuel.
3. **Find Meaning in the Mundane**–Pride in small tasks creates credibility for big ones.
4. **Own Your Mistakes**–Accountability builds trust. Blame destroys it.
5. **Lift Others Up**–True leaders create more leaders, not more followers.

The Forge of Leadership

To forge something means *to form or shape with concentrated effort*. That's leadership, formed under pressure, strengthened by heat, refined through experience.

Too many companies promote technical experts instead of people leaders. But leadership isn't about managing a process, it's about inspiring people.

The best crews I've ever seen didn't have the newest tools or the biggest budgets. They had trust, respect, and shared purpose.

Abel gets that. That's why he thrives.

Why This Matters Now

Our industry needs leaders who remember where they came from—leaders who haven't forgotten the calluses, the cold mornings, and the sweat equity that built their careers.

We need leaders who measure success not just in cubic yards or revenue, but in the growth, safety, and well-being of their people.

> - Because leadership isn't a promotion—it's a responsibility.
> - It's the quiet courage to step up when others step back.
> - It's the humility to lead with empathy, not ego.
> - And it's the determination to keep forging forward, no matter where you started.

The Final Pour

When I look back at my journey, from laborer to business owner, from worker to coach, I see the same truth reflected in Abel's story:

We didn't just build with concrete. We built **character**.

That's what leadership really is, showing others that where you start doesn't define where you'll finish.

So, whether you're holding a shovel or holding a meeting, remember this:

Leadership isn't a Title. It's a Transformation

It's forged in effort, strengthened by humility, and built one pour, one lesson, and one person at a time.

Just as metal is refined by heat and hammer, leadership is forged by experience and reflection. The more pressure you endure, the stronger your leadership becomes.

Leadership Builder

Ask yourself:

> ➢ What "forge moments" in my career changed how I lead?
>
> ➢ Who on my team is quietly showing leadership potential that I can mentor?

Section Two

OPERATIONAL EXCELLENCE

Chapter 9

SYSTEMS AND SOPS: THE GAME CHANGERS FOR CONSISTENCY

Structure doesn't limit leaders, it liberates them

The construction industry thrives on movement, with people, equipment, schedules, and expectations constantly shifting. Projects evolve, weather changes, and deadlines loom. In that kind of chaos, systems keep the ship steady. Written processes and SOPs aren't paperwork for the sake of compliance, they're the backbone of consistency, the quiet force that transforms good companies into great ones.

This chapter explores how structure and systems don't confine leadership; they create freedom. Freedom from confusion, rework, and the endless cycle of solving the same problems twice. When leaders invest in clear systems, they're not creating red tape, they're building runways for their people to succeed.

Why Structure Matters

In the early days of any company, structure feels optional. When a business is small, everyone wears multiple hats. People figure things out as they go. The owner is close enough to every project to catch mistakes before they grow. It's fast, flexible, and personal, and it works... until it doesn't.

Growth exposes the cracks. Suddenly, the same flexibility that once felt freeing becomes chaos. The same informality that once made the company feel tight-knit starts breeding confusion. You can't be everywhere at once anymore, and decisions that used to take seconds now take hours because no one is sure who's responsible, what the process is, or which version of the truth to trust.

That's where structure earns its value.

It doesn't replace leadership; it amplifies it.

Structure is Not Control—It's Clarity

Many leaders equate structure with bureaucracy. They worry it'll stifle initiative or creativity. But in truth, structure does the opposite, it removes the fog. It defines roles, outlines expectations, and makes accountability clear.

Without structure, employees spend their energy *figuring out what to do*. With structure, they spend it *doing the work*.

Structure gives people confidence. When every foreman knows how to start a job, how to close one out, and what "done right" looks like, they can lead without constant direction. Structure isn't about taking power away; it's about giving it to the right people at the right time.

Chaos is Not a Sign of Growth—It's a Sign of a Missing System

In construction, complexity is unavoidable: change orders, weather delays, shifting crews, and unpredictable suppliers are part of the game. But chaos is optional. Chaos shows up when structure doesn't.

When every project has its own "unwritten rules," the company becomes dependent on personalities instead of the processes. That's risky. Because when one key person leaves, takes vacation, or burns out, the system collapses.

Structure protects against that fragility. It ensures that knowledge doesn't live in one person's head; it lives in the company. The business becomes more resilient, more teachable, and more valuable because it's not built on memory or emotion. It's built on process.

Structure Liberates Leadership

The irony of leadership is that the more structured you become, the more freedom you gain.

When you're small and disorganized, you lead by reaction. You spend your days putting out fires, answering the same questions, and making the same decisions again and again. You're busy, but you're not growing.

Structure breaks that cycle. When your expectations are documented and your systems are clear, you stop being the bottleneck. Leaders who once spent their time explaining the same process can now spend that time developing people, building relationships, and thinking strategically.

Structure frees you to lead instead of manage.

Structure Protects Culture

One of the most overlooked reasons that structure matters is its connection to culture. The way your company operates, how it communicates, trains, and handles conflict, becomes the daily lived experience of your employees.

When expectations are vague, frustration takes root. People start blaming each other, cutting corners, and interpreting "the way we do things" differently. But when systems are clear and consistently applied, fairness becomes part of the culture. Accountability becomes normalized, not personal.

Written systems reinforce your values. They say, *this is who we are, and this is how we do things around here*. Over time, that consistency builds pride, trust, and belonging.

A strong culture isn't built from slogans; it's built from systems that live out those values on the jobsite.

Structure Makes the Invisible Visible

Every construction leader knows that what's measured improves. But what's unmeasured drifts.

Structure turns invisible habits into visible data. When processes are written, leaders can evaluate performance, track progress, and identify bottlenecks objectively. Problems stop being personal; they become solvable.

A structured environment allows for healthy accountability—not micromanagement, but clarity. It shifts conversations from *"Why didn't you do this?"* to *"Let's look at where the system broke down."* That single shift changes everything about how a team grows together.

Structure is the Foundation of Scalability

At its core, structure makes growth sustainable. Anyone can grow fast; few can grow well.

Without structure, growth multiplies inefficiency. Every project adds confusion. Every new employee inherits chaos. But with clear systems, every project becomes a replication of proven success.

It's like forming and pouring concrete: the formwork defines the shape. You can't pour without a structure to hold it. I mean, I guess you can, but it's going to look like hell! Systems are that formwork for your business, they give shape to your vision.

When you build strong forms, you can pour as much as you want, knowing it'll hold. That's the power of structure; it scales strength without losing shape.

The Leadership Shift

At some point in every company's journey, there's a moment when the owner realizes:

"I can't keep running it out of my head."

That's the turning point between being a doer and being a builder of builders. Structure allows that transformation. It's how you turn a good operator into a true leader, not because you've gained control, but because you've given it away, through systems that empower others to lead with clarity and consistency.

The Power of Written Systems

If leadership is about alignment, then systems are the tools that make alignment possible. A clear, well-written system transforms ideas into consistent action. It's the difference between "We know what to do" and "We all do it the same way."

Many companies operate by memory, habit, or verbal

tradition—A patchwork of "how Joe always does it." That might work when the company is small and the owner is everywhere, but it collapses under growth. Systems are how leaders multiply themselves. They capture wisdom and turn it into a playbook the whole team can run.

Consistency Builds Trust

Consistency is what turns good crews into great ones. When every operator, foreman, and project manager performs a task the same way, quality stops being a variable. Clients notice. Employees feel confident. Trust, both internal and external, becomes part of the company culture.

Inside the company, consistency creates psychological safety. Employees gain confidence when they know what's expected and how success is defined. They can focus on execution instead of second-guessing the process or trying to read their boss's mind.

A consistent process doesn't remove creativity; it gives it boundaries. Once people master the system, they can innovate *within* it. That's where excellence lives: predictable standards combined with individual ownership.

Efficiency Reduces Waste

A solid written system is like a well-oiled piece of equipment: smooth, reliable, and efficient. When teams know the order of operations, they spend less time debating next steps and more time executing them.

In construction, time is money. Every minute spent searching for forms, calling for clarification, or redoing work because of miscommunication eats into margins.

SOPs reduce those hidden costs. They clarify who does what, when, and how, so people don't waste energy on decisions that have already been made.

Well-built systems also allow for continuous improvement. Once a process is written, it can be measured and refined. You can't fix what you can't see; but when the system is visible, data replaces opinion, and improvement becomes part of the culture.

Reducing Errors and Protecting People

Human error is inevitable, but systems make it preventable. Written procedures act as guardrails; they catch small mistakes before they become costly problems.

A written pre-pour checklist can prevent a missed inspection that could delay a project. A documented maintenance process can prevent an injury. A clear communication protocol can stop safety hazards from going unreported.

Every error avoided through a well-designed system is time, money, and trust preserved. In safety-critical industries like construction and mining, that's not just good business, that's leadership in action.

Empowering Onboarding and Training

Most new hires learn through a form of organized chaos: shadowing someone, piecing together habits, and trying to survive. That's not training; that's trial by fire. Written systems change that.

They make onboarding repeatable, measurable, and fair. When new employees can reference documented steps, expectations, and visuals, they learn faster and with less frustration. Experienced workers appreciate it too; it frees them from reteaching the basics over and over.

Training tied to written SOPs also reinforces accountability. It's not "I didn't know," it's "Let's review the process." The standard becomes clear, and leaders can coach to it.

Scalability and Growth

Every company hits a point where growth turns from opportunity to overload, unless systems are in place. A single owner can manage 10 people by memory, but not 50. Growth magnifies inconsistency; and without systems, what once worked suddenly breaks.

Written systems make scaling possible. They allow a foreman in one region to run a crew the same way a foreman does three states away. They help new divisions operate with the same standards as the original location.

In short, systems replicate success. They create a framework for leadership to delegate confidently. When processes are clear and repeatable, leaders can spend their time developing people instead of putting out fires.

Improved Communication and Collaboration

In construction, miscommunication costs more than almost any other mistake. A single missed detail can derail a job.

Written systems create a shared language. When everyone uses the same forms, terminology, and reporting standards, misunderstandings drop dramatically. Field teams know what the office needs, project managers know what to expect, and clients see transparency in every step.

Systems, in the end, aren't about control; they're about connection. They connect people, processes, and purpose.

The Freedom That Structure Creates

Some leaders resist systems because they fear rigidity, they don't want to become bureaucratic or lose flexibility. But in truth, systems *create* freedom. When everyone understands the rules of the game, leaders don't have to micromanage.

Structure liberates leaders to focus on strategy, innovation, and people. It gives employees the confidence to make decisions within boundaries. And it ensures that excellence doesn't depend on any one person, it's built into the fabric of how the company operates.

Written systems are not just operational tools; they are leadership tools. They embody discipline, clarity, and accountability. They free you from running the business by memory and turn your expectations into execution.

When systems are alive and used daily, they stop being documents on a shelf and start becoming the DNA of your organization.

What Makes a System Work

Not all systems are created equal. A binder full of outdated checklists buried in a foreman's truck isn't helping anyone. Effective systems are simple, accessible, and alive.

1. **Clarity and Simplicity**–Write it like you're teaching a new apprentice. Straightforward language beats technical jargon every time.

2. **Step-by-Step Flow**–Outline processes clearly so there's no room for interpretation.
3. **Customization**–Fit the process to your company's reality, not someone else's template.
4. **Visuals**–Use flowcharts, photos, or screenshots where possible. One picture can save 10 paragraphs.
5. **Regular Updates**–Revisit each SOP at least annually. Technology and regulations evolve faster than we think, especially software systems.
6. **Easy Access**–Make systems accessible in the field. QR codes on equipment or digital SOP libraries can eliminate excuses.

Bringing Systems to Life

Rolling out systems isn't a one-and-done project. It's cultural. It requires leadership buy-in and consistent reinforcement.

Start by assessing what's broken and finding where the bottlenecks, miscommunications, or inconsistencies cost time or money. Involve your people in developing solutions so they have ownership. Pilot the process, train thoroughly, and refine as you go.

Systems aren't meant to live in binders; they're meant to breathe in daily operations.

A Case in Point

A mid-sized construction firm I worked with struggled with schedule delays and inconsistent quality. They had great people, but no documented processes. Every foreman ran jobs "their way."

We worked together to implement SOPs for site inspections, safety, and materials management. Within six months, timelines improved by 20%. Quality audits went up. Employee turnover went down. They didn't add people, they added clarity.

By capturing their best practices and making them repeatable, the company didn't just get more efficient; it became scalable. They were finally ready to grow.

The Long-Term Payoff

Written systems do more than solve today's problems, they build tomorrow's stability.

They **institutionalize knowledge**, ensuring that when a key employee leaves, their experience doesn't walk out the door.

They **enhance reputation**, because consistency builds credibility.

And they **protect compliance**, helping leaders sleep at night knowing their safety and operational standards are met.

Systems make your business teachable, transferable, and sustainable.

The Leadership Lesson

Leadership is tested in the gap between expectation and execution. Written systems close that gap. They turn vision into action and remove the guesswork from performance.

Great leaders don't micromanage; they document, train, and trust. They build systems so their people can win without constant supervision.

A company without written systems is building on sand. One with documented standards is building on bedrock.

Leadership Builder

Ask yourself:

➢ Where does inconsistency cost your team: time, safety, or trust?

➢ What process could you document today that would make tomorrow easier for someone else?

➢ How can you model the discipline you expect from your team when it comes to following systems?

Chapter 10

KEY KPIS: MEASURING WHAT MATTERS MOST

What gets measured shapes what gets mastered

Key Performance Indicators (KPIs) are critical metrics that help construction organizations monitor their progress, identify inefficiencies, and ensure they are meeting their goals. Measuring productivity, financial gain, and overall organizational health requires a combination of operational, financial, and strategic KPIs. Many organizations have this data readily available if they are using some sort of accounting software or job cost tracking software. This chapter outlines the most impactful KPIs for the construction industry and how they provide actionable insights to drive success.

Productivity KPIs

Productivity KPIs measure the efficiency of operations, ensuring projects stay on schedule and within budget.

Labor Productivity

Formula: (Total Output ÷ Total Labor Hours)
Example: XYZ Company places concrete by hand for an intersection. They placed 1,500 Square Yards (SY) utilizing 75 total labor hours. 1,500/75 = 20 SY Man Hours (MH)

> Total Output can be measured as total goods or services produced (e.g., GDP, total revenue, etc.).

> Total Hours Worked refers to the total number of hours worked by all employees or the workforce during a specific period

Purpose: Evaluates how efficiently the workforce is completing tasks, allowing managers to identify bottlenecks or inefficiencies.

Equipment Utilization Rate

Formula: (Equipment Actual Operating Hours ÷ Equipment Available Hours) × 100

Example: Your Excavator is being tracked for a month. There are typically 20 working days in a month (this varies depending on holidays, etc.) For this exercise, we will assume 10 hour working days resulting in 200 Available hours for the month. The excavator was used for 160 hours during the month. (160/200) × 100 = 80% utilization rate for the excavator.

> Actual Hours Used is the total number of hours the equipment was actually in use during a specific period.

> Available Hours is the total number of hours the equipment was available for use during that same period (often the number of hours the equipment is expected to be in operation)

Purpose: Measures how effectively machinery and equipment are being used, ensuring resources are not underutilized or overworked.

Project Schedule Variance (PSV)

Formula: Scheduled Completion Time – Actual Completion Time

Purpose: Tracks whether projects are ahead, behind, or on schedule. This helps identify areas where productivity improvements are needed.

Rework Rate

Formula: (Cost of Rework ÷ Total Project Cost) × 100

Purpose: Highlights the frequency of errors and their impact on productivity, enabling the organization to address quality control issues.

Employee Utilization Rate

Formula: (Billable Hours ÷ Total Hours Worked) × 100

Purpose: Monitors how effectively employees' time is allocated to productive, billable tasks.

Financial Gain KPIs

Financial KPIs assess the profitability and financial stability of the organization, helping leaders make informed decisions to ensure growth.

Gross Profit Margin

Formula: (Revenue – Direct Costs) ÷ Revenue × 100

Purpose: Indicates the profitability of projects after accounting for direct costs such as labor, equipment, and materials.

Net Profit Margin

Formula: (Net Profit ÷ Revenue) × 100

Purpose: Provides a comprehensive view of overall profitability, factoring in all expenses, including overhead and taxes.

Cost Variance (CV)

Formula: Budgeted Cost − Actual Cost

Purpose: Measures how well the organization is controlling costs, identifying whether projects are over or under budget.

Return on Investment (ROI)

Formula: (Net Profit ÷ Investment Cost) × 100

Purpose: Assesses the financial return on investments in equipment, technology, or new projects.

Accounts Receivable Turnover

Formula: Net Credit Sales ÷ Average Accounts
        Receivable

Purpose: Tracks how quickly the organization collects payments, ensuring healthy cash flow.

Cash Flow Forecasting Accuracy

Formula: (Forecasted Cash Flow − Actual Cash Flow) ÷
        Forecasted Cash Flow × 100

Purpose: Evaluates the reliability of cash flow predictions, which are essential for financial planning.

Organizational Health KPIs

These KPIs provide a holistic view of the organization's overall performance, ensuring it is well-positioned for long-term success.

Employee Satisfaction and Retention Rate

Formula: (Number of Employees Staying ÷ Total Employees) × 100

Purpose: Measures employee engagement and loyalty, which are critical for maintaining a productive and motivated workforce.

Safety Incident Rate

Formula: (Number of Incidents ÷ Total Work Hours) × 200,000

Purpose: Tracks workplace safety, a key factor in maintaining a healthy and compliant work environment.

Bid–Win Ratio

Formula: (Bids Won ÷ Total Bids Submitted) × 100

Purpose: Measures the effectiveness of the organization's bidding strategy, ensuring resources are allocated to high-value opportunities. This is particularly important during down economies where you find yourself up against a lot of bidders. An organization may need to strategize to find other opportunities to find profitable work and reduce this number.

Backlog Value

Formula: Total Value of Uncompleted Contracts

Purpose: Indicates future revenue potential and helps assess the sustainability of the project pipeline.

Operational Efficiency Ratio

Formula: (Operating Costs ÷ Revenue) × 100

Purpose: Evaluates how efficiently the organization converts operational expenses into revenue.

Integrating KPIs into Decision-Making

➢ **Automating KPI Tracking**

Use project management software, financial tools, or dashboards to automate data collection and analysis. This reduces the manual effort required and ensures real-time updates.

➢ **Benchmarking Performance**

Compare current KPIs to industry standards and historical data to identify areas of improvement.

➢ **Actionable Insights**

Use KPIs as a foundation for decision-making, focusing on areas that directly impact organizational goals. For example, if the rework rate is high, invest in quality control processes or employee training.

➢ **Periodic Reviews**

Schedule regular KPI reviews to track progress and adapt strategies as needed.

Conclusion

In construction, measuring productivity, financial gain, and organizational health is essential for staying competitive and achieving long-term success. By identifying and tracking the right KPIs, organizations can gain actionable insights, optimize performance, and make informed decisions that drive growth and profitability. These metrics not only highlight current strengths and weaknesses but also provide a roadmap for continuous improvement and sustainability. From my experience, KPIs are most often overlooked by smaller contractors. Yet if one were to look at the numbers and find a few simple areas to improve which in turn add to the bottom line, shouldn't you do it? Yes, tracking and measuring operational effectiveness isn't just for big companies, it's for companies of all sizes!

Key Performance Indicators aren't just numbers, they're leadership tools. Metrics tell the story of how well your vision translates into reality. Great leaders don't just track data; they interpret it, coach through it, and align their teams around it. When you lead with insight instead of instinct, you turn information into influence.

Leadership Builder

Ask yourself:

> ➢ Which KPI best reflects the health of my leadership, profit, retention, or engagement?
> ➢ How can I use data to start better conversations with my team instead of ending them?
> ➢ Do my people understand how their daily effort connects to the results we measure?

Chapter 11

THE 5% CHALLENGE

Leading Through Continuous Improvement

Big results are built through small, consistent improvements.

In construction, where profit margins can be razor-thin, the difference between success and struggle often comes down to small efficiencies. While massive overhauls grab attention, addressing just 5% of waste in operations, materials, or time can yield significant financial and operational benefits. This chapter explores how identifying and eliminating 5% waste impacts your bottom line, the areas to examine, and actionable strategies to achieve this transformation.

The Power of Small Changes

Success in construction rarely comes from one massive breakthrough. It's built brick by brick, improvement by improvement. When we focus on reducing waste and inefficiency by just 5%, the compounding effect can be extraordinary.

Compounding Gains

Eliminating 5% of waste in multiple areas adds up quickly. Over time, these small efficiencies create exponential growth. For example, reducing material waste by 5% across several projects might seem insignificant in isolation, but over a year that improvement could save thousands, or even millions, of dollars.

Boosting Margins

Even a small reduction in waste protects profit margins from volatility. Rising material costs, weather delays, or unexpected rework can easily erode profits; but a leaner operation creates a financial buffer. That 5% can mean the difference between barely breaking even and achieving a healthy return.

Gaining a Competitive Edge

Efficiency becomes a strategic advantage. Companies that learn to operate leaner can bid more competitively, deliver faster, and still maintain profitability. In a market where everyone is chasing the same contracts, the company that masters small, continuous improvement wins more often, and sustains its success longer.

Understanding the 5% of Waste

Every construction project contains hidden inefficiencies. They often go unnoticed because they're woven into the fabric of daily operations, routine delays, overlooked materials, small mistakes, or unclear communication. Yet collectively, they drain time, money, and morale.

Waste takes many forms:

> **Material Waste:** Overordering, mishandling, or improper storage that leads to damage or loss.

- ➢ **Time Waste:** Downtime from scheduling conflicts, unproductive meetings, or excessive rework.
- ➢ **Labor Inefficiencies:** Miscommunication, lack of training, or underutilization of talent.
- ➢ **Process Waste:** Outdated workflows or redundant steps that slow progress without adding value.

Individually, these issues might seem minor, but together they can erode profits and compromise timelines. Tackling just 5% of this waste is a realistic and powerful place to begin.

Identifying Waste: The First Step

The key to tackling the 5% Challenge is systematic identification. You can't fix what you don't see. Start by assessing your construction processes from pre-construction planning to project delivery. Here's how to uncover areas of waste:

- ➢ **Data Analysis:** Use project data to identify trends in overruns, material usage, and productivity. Are there recurring patterns of inefficiency?
- ➢ **Site Audits:** Conduct on-site observations to pinpoint where time, materials, or labor are being misused.
- ➢ **Employee Feedback:** Engage workers at all levels to understand bottlenecks and frustrations they face daily.
- ➢ **Technology Assessment:** Evaluate whether outdated tools or software are contributing to delays or errors. By breaking down operations into manageable components, waste becomes easier to detect.

Correcting the Waste

Once you've identified the waste, the next step is implementing targeted solutions. These interventions don't need to be radical; small adjustments can yield significant savings.

- ➢ **Optimize Material Usage:** Implement just-in-time delivery systems and monitor inventory closely to minimize overordering and reduce spoilage.
- ➢ **Improve Scheduling:** Use advanced scheduling software to ensure efficient use of equipment and labor while avoiding downtime.
- ➢ **Enhance Communication:** Adopt digital tools that provide real-time updates, reducing delays caused by miscommunication.
- ➢ **Streamline Workflows:** Conduct process mapping exercises to eliminate redundant steps or align tasks more effectively.
- ➢ **Invest in Training:** Equip your workforce with the skills and knowledge to perform their roles efficiently and reduce costly errors.

The Ripple Effect on Your Bottom Line

Eliminating 5% of waste doesn't just save money, it has a cascading impact on profitability. Here's how:

- ➢ **Cost Savings:** Reduced material waste, fewer delays, and streamlined processes directly cut expenses.
- ➢ **Increased Productivity:** With fewer inefficiencies, workers can complete tasks faster and with higher quality.

- ➢ **Enhanced Reputation:** Delivering projects on time and within budget strengthens your brand and builds trust with clients.
- ➢ **Competitive Advantage:** Lower costs and higher efficiency position your firm to win more bids at competitive prices.

Building a Culture of Efficiency

The 5% Challenge is more than a one-time initiative; it's the foundation of a culture of continuous improvement. Encourage your team to embrace this mindset by:

- ➢ **Setting Clear Goals:** Regularly define achievable efficiency targets and celebrate progress.
- ➢ **Promoting Transparency:** Share performance data and lessons learned across teams to foster accountability and collaboration.
- ➢ **Empowering Employees:** Give workers the tools and authority to suggest and implement improvements.
- ➢ **Recognizing Success:** Highlight and reward individuals or teams who contribute to waste reduction efforts.

Example

Consider a mid-size construction firm that adopted the 5% Challenge. Through detailed analysis, they discovered inefficiencies in material handling, with over 8% of their budget tied up in waste. By implementing smarter procurement practices and improving storage solutions, they reduced material waste by 5.5%. This change alone translated into $120,000 in annual savings, which they reinvested into training and equipment upgrades. Within a year, overall project profitability improved by 15%, demonstrating the power of small, targeted improvements.

Conclusion

The 5% Challenge isn't about perfection, it's about progress. By consistently targeting incremental gains, construction firms can unlock hidden potential, improve margins, and future-proof their operations. Start small, stay consistent, and watch how the ripple effects transform your business.

More importantly, the 5% Challenge is not just a cost-saving initiative, it's a mindset shift. It changes how you see your work, your team, and your leadership. By identifying and correcting even small inefficiencies in materials, time, labor, and processes, you create more than financial benefit—you build a stronger, more resilient organization. These incremental improvements ripple outward, fostering a culture of accountability, precision, and teamwork that elevates your entire operation.

Success in construction doesn't come from sweeping overnight changes. It comes from steady, intentional improvement, one small step at a time. By tackling just 5% waste, you position your company for long-term profitability and sustainable growth in a competitive industry.

I can't stress this enough: the 5% Challenge is more than a metric; it's a mindset. Great leaders look for small, sustainable gains that compound over time. When you challenge your team to find just 5% more efficiency, safety, or quality each week, you inspire ownership, creativity, and pride. That mindset transforms culture from *"good enough"* to *"how can we make it better?"*

Take the challenge. Engage your team. Lead by example. Because when small improvements become habits, excellence becomes inevitable.

Leadership Builder

Ask yourself:

- ➤ What 5% improvement could transform my leadership or organization?
- ➤ How can I celebrate small wins to reinforce continuous improvement?
- ➤ What barriers prevent my team from speaking up with better ideas?

Chapter 12

ROLES AND RESPONSIBILITIES

Clarity Builds Confidence

Clarity is kindness, especially in leadership.

In the construction industry—where projects involve multiple teams, tight timelines, and complex processes—clarity is key. Written roles and responsibilities are essential to creating a well-organized and efficient work environment. Without clearly defined duties, miscommunication, duplication of effort, and costly mistakes arise. This chapter explores why documenting roles and responsibilities is critical and how it can elevate performance, morale, and the overall success of your construction organization.

Why Written Roles and Responsibilities Matter

In construction, clarity is everything. Just as a project can't begin without a blueprint, a team can't perform at its best without clearly defined roles and responsibilities. Written documentation removes the guesswork. When everyone knows exactly what's expected of them, how their performance is measured, and how their work connects to the larger mission, accountability naturally follows. People take more ownership when they know where they fit and how success is defined.

Without written clarity, confusion creeps in. In a busy jobsite or office, overlapping duties and vague expectations lead to wasted time, duplicated efforts, and frustration. Clear documentation eliminates ambiguity. It ensures every task has an owner and that no one steps on another's toes, or worse, assumes someone else is handling it. This structure not only keeps work organized but also strengthens collaboration, because people can focus on doing their jobs instead of figuring out who's responsible for what.

Defined roles also streamline communication. When responsibilities are written and understood, teams know exactly who to contact for decisions, approvals, or solutions. This prevents bottlenecks, reduces downtime, and minimizes the endless back-and-forth that often plagues construction projects. Instead of guessing, people can get answers faster, which leads to smoother coordination and stronger results.

Efficiency improves when everyone stays in their lane. Employees can focus on their specific duties without distractions or unnecessary involvement in unrelated tasks. That focus boosts productivity, lowers stress, and keeps the job moving forward. Over time, this discipline translates directly into profitability.

There's also a compliance advantage. Written roles and responsibilities protect both the company and its employees by showing clear delegation of duties, authority, and accountability. In industries as regulated as construction, this documentation helps ensure compliance with OSHA standards, labor laws, and contractual obligations. If a dispute or audit ever arises, written clarity becomes your best defense; it shows due diligence and proper oversight.

Clarity in roles doesn't just improve workflow, it improves morale. People perform better when they understand their purpose. When employees know what's expected and how their efforts contribute to the team's success, confidence and engagement rise. Frustration fades, retention increases, and the organization develops a stronger sense of unity and pride.

Written responsibilities also make scaling your business easier. As you grow, you can onboard new hires faster and maintain consistency across crews or departments. Defined roles become a framework for growth, allowing you to expand operations without losing control or culture.

Key Elements of Effective Role Documentation

A well-crafted description of the role should paint a clear picture of what success looks like in that position. Start with a **clear title and overview**, a short summary of why the role exists, and how it contributes to the company's mission. Then outline the **core responsibilities**, listing the key duties and expectations with enough detail to eliminate ambiguity.

Define the **reporting structure**, noting who the individual reports to, who reports to them, and any cross-functional collaboration required. Clarify **decision-making authority**: what can be handled independently versus what requires approval. Then set **performance expectations**—measurable outcomes such as productivity goals, quality standards, or timelines.

Don't forget the **skills and qualifications** needed to perform the job well, including education, certifications, or technical expertise. Finally, include **safety and compliance responsibilities**, especially for field positions. In construction, safety isn't just a priority, it's a core value, and to define that in writing reinforces accountability from day one.

How to Implement Written Roles and Responsibilities

Start by conducting a **role analysis**. Talk with employees and managers to understand what each position truly entails, not just what's on paper. Collaboration is key. Involving team members in the process ensures accuracy, builds buy-in, and reveals the real pain points that might otherwise go unnoticed.

Once you've gathered input, **draft clear and comprehensive descriptions**. Use direct language and avoid vague, generic statements. Be specific about duties, decision-making authority, and expectations. Then, **review and approve** the documents with leadership or HR to ensure they align with organizational goals and policies.

After approval, **communicate and distribute** the documents to your team. These shouldn't live in a file drawer; they should be referenced regularly during onboarding, training, and performance reviews. Written roles work only when they're understood and applied.

Lastly, **review and update regularly**. Construction is a dynamic industry, and roles evolve as projects, technologies, and regulations change. Schedule periodic reviews to keep documents accurate and relevant. Integrate these written expectations into ongoing training and leadership development programs so that clarity becomes part of your culture, not just your paperwork.

When everyone knows their role, communication improves, efficiency rises, and leadership becomes easier. Written roles and responsibilities aren't bureaucracy; they're blueprints for accountability. In an industry built on plans and precision, it only makes sense that our people deserve the same.

Blueprints build projects; clarity builds people.

Benefits Beyond the Jobsite

Clear roles and responsibilities do more than streamline operations; they contribute to a positive organizational culture. Employees are more likely to feel respected and motivated when their roles are clearly defined, and leaders can focus on strategic goals rather than resolving preventable conflicts. In addition, written roles help build a foundation for innovation. With less ambiguity, teams can focus their energy on improving processes, adopting new technologies, and achieving higher levels of performance.

Diving Deeper into the Importance of Written Roles and Responsibilities

In the construction industry, written roles and responsibilities go beyond basic organization; they create the framework for effective leadership, accountability, and growth. In the next section, we'll expand on their value by exploring their impact on critical aspects of a construction organization, common pitfalls when roles are unclear, and actionable ways to leverage role clarity for long-term success.

The Expanded Impact of Written Roles and Responsibilities

In the world of construction and project management, success often hinges on one fundamental principle: clarity. When every team member knows exactly what they're responsible for, and more importantly, what they're *not* responsible for, the entire organization operates with greater precision and trust. Written roles and responsibilities are more than HR formalities; they are blueprints for accountability, communication, and performance.

Improved Project Management

Construction projects are intricate operations involving dozens of moving parts, managers, subcontractors, suppliers, inspectors, and more. Without clear definitions of who does what, confusion can spread quickly and productivity suffers. Written roles act as a roadmap for coordination, ensuring that every task, from budgeting to site supervision, has an owner.

For example, when a project manager's role explicitly includes progress reporting and budget tracking, and the site supervisor oversees daily operations, there's no risk of overlap or neglect. Each person can stay in their lane, while understanding how their performance affects the broader project.

Enhanced Accountability and Trust

Defined roles create a culture of accountability. When responsibilities are clear, there's no need for finger-pointing or excuses. People naturally have ownership because expectations are transparent. This not only builds trust across teams but also reinforces reliability within leadership.

Consider the foreman who knows it's their duty to enforce safety measures on-site. They don't assume someone else will handle hazards; they act, because the responsibility is written, understood, and expected. That clarity transforms accountability from a reactive behavior into a proactive habit.

Streamlined Decision-Making

Unclear authority is one of the biggest bottlenecks in fast-paced industries like construction. Written roles define decision-making boundaries, empowering employees to take action within their scope without hesitation or unnecessary approval loops.

When a procurement officer knows they can approve purchases up to a certain dollar limit, decisions are made real-time, not lost in managerial traffic. The result is a more agile organization that meets deadlines and reduces costly delays.

Cross-Team Collaboration

Clear roles don't create silos; they break them down. When employees understand how their work intersects with others, collaboration becomes natural. Teams begin to see the full picture, not just their individual tasks.

For instance, a site engineer who collaborates with a quality assurance manager will better understand how design modifications affect inspection standards. This mutual clarity strengthens communication between departments and ensures everyone is working toward the same goal.

Risk Mitigation

In construction, unclear roles can lead to much more than inefficiency, they can create real danger. Missed tasks, forgotten safety checks, or misunderstood procedures can result in accidents, non-compliance, or project delays. Documented roles reduce these risks by assigning ownership where it matters most.

During a concrete pour, for example, a quality control technician who knows they're responsible for verifying the mix against specifications is far more likely to catch a mistake before it becomes a costly problem. Clear roles protect not just the schedule and budget, but lives.

The Dangers of Unclear Roles and Responsibilities

The absence of clarity has predictable consequences. When no one knows exactly who owns what, chaos takes root. Efforts are duplicated, deadlines are missed, and quality begins to slip. Over time, morale declines as frustration replaces focus.

Duplication of effort wastes valuable resources as multiple people unknowingly tackle the same task. Missed deadlines follow, often because everyone assumed someone else was handling it. The result is a demoralized team working in confusion, where inconsistent quality and internal conflict become the norm. Overlapping responsibilities eventually breed resentment, undermining teamwork, and eroding trust—the very foundation of a safe and productive jobsite.

Implementing Written Roles and Responsibilities Effectively

Establishing written roles isn't a one-time exercise; it's an evolving process that requires thoughtful planning and continuous attention.

The first step is to conduct an organizational assessment. Then map out how work currently flows and identify where responsibilities overlap or fall through the cracks. These problem areas reveal opportunities to clarify and streamline operations.

Once the big picture is clear, define roles around key functions: project management, site supervision, safety enforcement, procurement, quality control, and so on. Involve employees directly in the drafting process. The best insights often come from the people doing the work every day, and their input ensures the roles accurately reflect real-world expectations.

For complex projects, use structured tools like RACI (Responsible, Accountable, Consulted, Informed) matrices. These frameworks visually display who owns each part of a task, who needs to be consulted, and who must stay informed—eliminating gray areas before they cause trouble.

Next, make these definitions accessible. Document each role in a centralized system or employee handbook that's easy for everyone to find. Reinforce these expectations during onboarding, team meetings, and performance reviews so clarity becomes part of your company's rhythm.

Finally, connect responsibilities to measurable outcomes. When each role ties directly to KPIs, employees understand the tangible impact of their work. Schedule periodic reviews to ensure these descriptions stay relevant as the company grows or project scopes evolve.

Written roles and responsibilities may seem simple, but they're one of the most powerful tools for building a culture of accountability, safety, and efficiency. In construction, as in leadership, clarity isn't just a management tool. It's a competitive advantage.

Examples of Written Roles and Responsibilities in Action

Example 1: Role Definition for a Construction Superintendent

Job Title: Construction Superintendent

Overview: Oversee daily on-site operations to ensure

projects are completed on schedule, within budget, and in compliance with safety and quality standards.

Core Responsibilities:

- ➤ Manage subcontractors and crew assignments.
- ➤ Monitor daily progress and report to the project manager.
- ➤ Enforce site safety protocols and compliance with regulations.
- ➤ Coordinate material deliveries to prevent delays.
- ➤ Conduct regular inspections to maintain quality standards.

Example 2: Role Definition for a Safety Officer

Job Title: Safety Officer

Overview: Ensure workplace safety by implementing and monitoring safety protocols and procedures.

Core Responsibilities:

- ➤ Conduct regular safety audits and inspections.
- ➤ Deliver safety training and toolbox talks to crews.
- ➤ Investigate and document workplace accidents.
- ➤ Maintain compliance with OSHA and other safety regulations.
- ➤ Collaborate with site supervisors to address potential hazards.

Additional Benefits of Written Roles

1. **Improved Hiring Processes**
   Accurate role descriptions help HR teams and

recruiters attract candidates with the right skills and experience.

2. **Facilitates Career Growth**

   Employees can see a clear pathway for advancement within the organization when roles and responsibilities are well-defined.

3. **Supports Succession Planning**

   Documented roles make it easier to train and transition new employees into key positions, reducing downtime when turnover occurs.

Conclusion

Clear, written roles and responsibilities are a cornerstone of any successful construction organization. They ensure clarity, accountability, and efficiency, allowing teams to work together seamlessly and achieve project goals. When roles are well-documented, employees feel confident, valued, and empowered to perform their best work. In an industry where egos and tempers flare, taking the time to define and communicate roles isn't just a best practice; it's a competitive advantage.

By investing the time to define and document these roles, your organization can reduce risks, improve morale, and create a solid framework for sustainable growth. Clear roles and responsibilities aren't just about assigning tasks, they are about empowering people to succeed and contributing to the overall health of your organization. By embracing this approach, you set your organization up for sustained growth, improved morale, and long-term success.

Ambiguity kills performance. When people aren't sure where their lane is, they hesitate, overlap, or collide. Written roles and responsibilities remove that confusion and replace it with confidence. Leaders who provide clarity earn trust, and teams that understand expectations operate with purpose and pride.

Leadership Builder

Ask yourself:

> ➢ Does everyone on my team know what success looks like in their role?
>
> ➢ How often do I revisit and realign responsibilities as the company evolves?
>
> ➢ Where might unclear expectations be creating friction or frustration?

Chapter 13

LETTING GO

Trusting the Process and the People

If you can't let go, you can't grow.

Leadership has many inflection points, moments where the choice to hold on or to release will determine the future trajectory of your company, your team, and even your own wellbeing. Letting go does not mean abandoning responsibility or lowering standards; it means shifting from doing to leading, from controlling every detail to empowering others to rise. It's a discipline, a mindset, and in many ways a test of who you are becoming as a leader.

Most leaders don't struggle with letting go because they're weak; they struggle because they care. They care about the work. They care about the customer. They care about the reputation they've spent years, sometimes decades, building. For many, letting go feels like loosening their grip on the very thing that has kept their business alive. And yet, paradoxically, that same tight grip often becomes the bottleneck that limits growth, scalability, and sanity.

I know this firsthand. Over the years—in construction, leadership, safety consulting, and now Freedom Forge— I've had countless moments where I realized I was my own bottleneck. I cared so deeply about the work being excellent that I convinced myself I needed to be hands-on in every corner of the operation. And like most leaders who reach that point, I eventually learned that holding onto everything doesn't make you effective; it makes you exhausted. It stifles your team, slows the organization, and keeps you trapped at a level beneath your potential.

Letting go is one of the most important leadership skills you will ever learn. And once mastered, it becomes one of the most freeing.

Why Letting Go is So Hard

Letting go isn't a simple behavioral adjustment; it's a psychological shift. The resistance leaders feel toward delegating or releasing control is rooted in deeper patterns, identity, fear, expectations, and conditioning that often go unexamined.

Fear of Failure

When you're responsible for people, projects, safety, profitability, and reputation, the stakes feel heavy. Leaders often assume that by delegating, they're opening the door to mistakes; mistakes they'll ultimately be accountable for. Fear is a powerful motivator, and when it comes to delegation, it often shows up disguised as "I'll just do it myself."

One of my coaches, once shared the acronym FEAR: **False Expectations Appearing Real**. That stuck with me. When leaders imagine everything that could go wrong, they create a mental world where letting go automatically equals failure. But that expectation is rarely grounded in reality. More often, it's rooted in a belief programmed over years of feeling responsible for everything.

The truth is, refusing to let go is far riskier. Because when everything is on your shoulders, the system collapses the moment you step away, or worse, the moment you burn out.

Perfectionism

Many leaders quietly believe, "No one can do this as well as I can." And sometimes, early on, that might even be true. You built the work. You created the processes. You know the standard inside and out.

But leadership requires an upgrade in mindset: *the goal is no longer to be the best doer, but to build others who can do the work exceptionally well.*

Perfectionism is the silent killer of delegation. It convinces leaders to hand off a task, only to take it back the moment it's done "wrong." And nothing breaks trust faster than a leader who says, "I believe in you," then immediately snatches the work back because it wasn't done exactly their way.

When you correct someone's work without context, coaching, or collaboration, you don't just redo the task, you undo the trust.

Identity Tied to Work

For some leaders, their value has been tied to being indispensable. Their work ethic won them promotions. Their ability to produce results made them stand out. And when they built their business, being everywhere and doing everything felt like a badge of honor.

But identity evolves. At some point, your job stops being about how many tasks you can personally complete and becomes about how many people you can equip, empower, and elevate.

A shift happens when you ask yourself:

Would I rather be the hero of every task... or the leader of a high-performing team?

Your identity must grow from "the one who does the work" to "the one who leads the people who do the work." This shift is the beginning of freedom— freedom for your time, your family, your creativity, and your health. As my coach Admiral John "Boomer" Stufflebeem once told me, *"Time off is an investment in future productivity."* Most leaders don't realize how true, and how necessary that is.

Lack of Trust

Trust doesn't appear overnight; it's built through expectations, consistency, training, and accountability. But some leaders never give trust a chance to grow because they never take the first step.

You cannot trust someone to do something they've never been given the opportunity to do.

Trust is not only a leadership requirement; it's a leadership skill. You have to practice it. Start by giving away something small. Something that would relieve you, help them grow, and wouldn't break the company if it went wrong. Trust grows in layers: a small win makes the next handoff easier, and before long, the muscle of delegation becomes second nature.

Cultural Expectations

Our society often teaches leaders that being the busiest person in the room equals being the most valuable. Many business owners fall into the habit of being the first to arrive, the last to leave, and the one picking up every loose end because "that's what leaders do."

But leadership is not measured in hours logged. It's measured in impact created.

Hard work is expected, but only the right kind of hard work. Grinding without purpose makes you tired. Grinding on the wrong things makes you trapped. But investing deeply in the work that only you can do? That's where your value multiplies.

Why Letting Go Matters

Holding onto everything might feel like safeguarding the business, but it produces the opposite effect. The longer you hold onto control, the more you limit the growth of the company and the growth of the people inside it.

It Empowers Your Team

Delegation is one of the most powerful tools you have for developing people. When you trust someone with meaningful work, you signal that you believe in their capability and potential. Ownership fuels pride. Pride fuels performance. Performance fuels culture.

When people are empowered, they don't just complete tasks, they think, innovate, and rise.

It Frees You to Lead Strategically

If you're always stuck in the daily operations, reacting to problems and handling tasks others could manage, you cannot think long-term. You cannot innovate. You cannot create new opportunities. You cannot build relationships.

Letting go gives you back the bandwidth required for the work only you can do:

- ➢ Vision
- ➢ Strategy
- ➢ Critical decisions
- ➢ Culture
- ➢ Growth
- ➢ Partnerships
- ➢ High-level problem solving.

The work that moves the company forward is rarely found in your inbox. It's found in the space delegation creates.

It Builds Organizational Resilience

A team that relies entirely on the leader to make decisions is fragile. A team empowered to think and act independently is resilient. When leaders let go, they create depth: multiple people capable of stepping up, solving problems, and adapting when challenges arise.

The strongest companies don't depend on one person. They depend on a culture of shared ownership.

It Prevents Burnout

Leaders often underestimate how much their energy fuels the organization. When you're exhausted, overextended, stretched thin, or constantly stressed, everyone feels it: your employees, customers, partners, even your family.

Letting go is not a luxury. It is a responsibility.

When you delegate and empower, you give yourself permission to rest. To recharge. To think. To enjoy the life that you've built. You come back sharper, clearer, more focused, and far more effective.

It Builds a Culture of Trust

When you demonstrate trust, your team learns to trust each other. A culture of trust becomes a competitive advantage—employees stay longer, perform higher, and feel more committed to the mission. People don't leave companies where they feel trusted. They leave companies where they feel controlled.

How to Learn to Let Go

Letting go is not an instant transformation; it's practice. Like physical training or mastering a trade, it requires reps. Leaders who have spent years holding tightly must intentionally work to unlearn old habits and replace them with new ones.

The journey becomes far easier when you break it into steps.

Start Small

Don't begin by delegating your highest-stakes tasks. Choose one small responsibility that drains your time, but doesn't require your expertise. Hand it off with clarity and support. Then observe, not with judgment, but with curiosity.

This is where trust begins.

Set Clear Expectations

Letting go doesn't mean stepping back and hoping for the best. Effective delegation is rooted in clarity, clear goals, clear timelines, clear standards, and clear communication. When people know exactly what success looks like, they can rise to the occasion with confidence. When expectations are vague, people hesitate, second-guess themselves, or constantly check in for reassurance.

> ➢ Leaders often mistake clarity for micromanagement. It's not.
> ➢ Micromanagement is controlling every step.
> ➢ Clarity is defining the destination while giving your team freedom in how they get there.

When you handoff a task, answer the questions your team will naturally have:

> ➢ What does success look like?
> ➢ What's the deadline?
> ➢ What resources can I use?
> ➢ What constraints do I need to follow?
> ➢ What authority do I have to make decisions?

Providing this upfront reduces confusion, builds trust, and eliminates unnecessary back-and-forth. It also frees you from needing to check in constantly, because you've already established the roadmap.

Focus on Outcomes, Not Methods

This is one of the most difficult shifts for leaders to embrace. We all naturally gravitate toward the methods we've used in the past, especially when those methods helped us succeed. But when you judge your team on *how* they complete the work, instead of the quality of the results, you stifle their creativity and confidence.

There are many ways to complete a task effectively. Your way is not the only way.

If someone can achieve the right outcome safely, ethically, and efficiently, let them do it their way. Some of your company's best innovations will come from people who approached a task differently than you ever would have. Great leaders build an environment where creativity is welcomed, not restricted.

Invest in Training

One of the reasons leaders hesitate to delegate is the fear that their team isn't ready. Training solves that problem. When people know how to perform a task, they perform with confidence. Competence reduces fear, for both the leader and the employee.

> ➤ Training is not an expense.
> ➤ It's the down payment on future freedom.

When you invest in training your people, you're not just developing skills, you're building trust, capability, and culture. You're also creating more leaders. And leaders who grow leaders create organizations that thrive long after the original founder steps away.

Practice Patience

Letting go requires patience, especially early on. Mistakes will happen. Miscommunication will happen. Slow progress will happen. And that's okay.

> ➤ Your job isn't to prevent mistakes, it's to teach through them.
> ➤ Your job isn't to eliminate risk, it's to manage it.
> ➤ Your job isn't to make everything perfect, it's to make everything better.

When you intervene too quickly, you rob your team of the opportunity to learn. When you give them time and guidance, you equip them with skills they'll use long after you're out of the picture. Patience is the bridge between delegation and development. And for many leaders, it's the hardest bridge to cross.

Create Feedback Loops

Delegation isn't a one-and-done handoff. It requires rhythm. Connection. Conversation. A simple check-in can prevent confusion, misalignment, or frustration. But it's important that check-ins don't turn into micro-checks—constant interruptions that send the message "I don't trust you."

Healthy feedback loops focus on:

> ➤ Progress
> ➤ Roadblocks

➢ Needs
➢ Wins
➢ Adjustments

When these conversations happen consistently, your team improves faster, and your trust grows stronger. Feedback is not criticism. It is reinforcement. It is alignment. It is accountability. And when done well, it becomes one of your most powerful leadership tools.

Delegate Decision-Making Authority

Delegating tasks is good. Delegating decisions is transformational.

When people have the authority to make decisions within certain boundaries, they become more invested, more confident, and more capable. They start thinking like owners instead of employees. They begin solving problems instead of reporting them. They bring solutions instead of excuses.

➢ Decision-making authority is the ultimate vote of trust.
➢ And when people feel trusted, they rise.

Give them limits. Give them clarity. But most importantly, give them room to lead.

A Real-World Example of Letting Go

A project manager at a growing construction firm found himself stuck in the same cycle many leaders experience: long nights, early mornings, and endless pressure. Despite having a capable team, he handled nearly every operational detail himself: reviewing submittals, rewriting schedules, adjusting manpower, triple-checking budgets, and fielding every minor question. His team felt underutilized and disengaged because every meaningful decision ran through him.

He wasn't a bad leader. He was simply a leader who hadn't learned to let go.

As the company expanded, the cracks began to show. Deadlines slipped. Team members became frustrated. He felt overwhelmed. And eventually, he realized that the very thing he believed keeping the company together, his constant involvement, was actually holding it back.

He made a shift. Not overnight, but step by step.

He started by delegating small tasks, daily logs, material tracking, and subcontractor communication. Then he began assigning ownership over entire scopes of work. He invested in weekly training sessions, built clear expectations, and held structured check-ins instead of constant interruptions.

- ➢ Six months later, everything had changed.
- ➢ The team was performing independently, deadlines improved, and morale climbed.
- ➢ The project manager, now free to focus on planning, budgeting, and strategy, became more effective and far less stressed.
- ➢ The culture shifted from dependency to shared ownership.
- ➢ And all of it started with letting go.

Conclusion: Letting Go to Lead Better and Build a More Profitable Company

Letting go isn't about losing control, it's about transferring responsibility in a healthy, intentional way that strengthens your entire organization. It's about stepping fully into the role of leader instead of worker. And it's about building a company that doesn't rely on your constant involvement to survive.

When you let go, you gain:

- ➢ Space to think
- ➢ Time to rest
- ➢ Energy to innovate
- ➢ The ability to lead strategically
- ➢ The freedom to enjoy the life you've worked for.

True leadership isn't measured by how much you personally carry, but by how many people you empower to carry with you. Delegation is not a sign of weakness; it is the forge where future leaders are shaped. When you release control, you create space for others to rise, and in doing so, you amplify your own impact.

Letting go is the moment you stop being the ceiling of your company, and start being its multiplier.

Leadership Builder

Ask yourself:

- ➢ What responsibilities am I still holding that someone else could handle?

➢ Is my hesitation rooted in the lack of trust or fear of losing control?

➢ Who on my team deserves a chance to lead something new this quarter?

Chapter 14

MANAGING YOUR EMOTIONS

The Leader's Inner Discipline

It happened on a rain-soaked morning; one of those days where every instinct tells you the jobsite should be quiet. Gray skies, wet ground, puddles forming in the low spots. The kind of morning when any seasoned leader knows productivity will be questionable at best.

I remember stepping outside and noticing something that didn't add up: company trucks rolling toward the shop, crews making the long commute in, headlights cutting through the drizzle. Most of these guys lived an hour to an hour and a half away. On a rainy day, that's a long drive for a short, uncertain window of work.

- Concern shot through me.
- Fuel costs.
- Lost time.
- The inefficiency of getting tools out only to pack them back up.
- By the time the crews arrived, if the weather even cleared, it would be close to noon. Half a day gone.

I marched straight toward our Operations Manager and asked, with more edge in my voice than clarity in my thinking:

"What is going on? Why are all the guys on their way in?"

I had every legitimate business reason to question it. The concern was valid. The timing was valid. The cost was valid. But the way I approached that conversation wasn't.

> ➤ I didn't pause.
> ➤ I didn't ask questions.
> ➤ I didn't maintain composure.
> ➤ I reacted emotionally and I overstepped authority that had already been delegated.

The real issue that morning wasn't the weather.

> ➤ It wasn't the crews.
> ➤ It wasn't the drive time or the lost hours.

The real issue was my **emotional response**, my tone, my urgency, my frustration, and the way I let the moment override my leadership. In my concern, I stepped into someone else's lane and created confusion and tension where there didn't need to be any.

That moment taught me something I have never forgotten:

A leader can be right and still be wrong.

> ➤ Because leadership isn't just about decisions.
> ➤ It's about discipline.
> ➤ It's about how you show up when the unexpected hits.
> ➤ It's about controlling the emotional tone you bring into the room.

And that lesson leads directly to the truth that shapes this entire chapter:

The calmest voice in the chaos is the one people follow.

Introduction

Construction is an industry built on pressure, tight timelines, tighter margins, unpredictable weather, supply delays, client expectations, workforce challenges, and the everyday reality that one small misstep can ripple across an entire project. In an environment like that, emotions can run high. But leadership isn't measured by how you perform when everything is going right. Leadership shows when everything is going wrong, and people turn to you to see how *you* respond.

Your emotional discipline becomes the emotional climate of your organization.

> ➤ A calm leader creates calm teams.
> ➤ A frantic leader creates frantic teams.
> ➤ An angry leader creates fearful teams.
> ➤ A patient leader creates confident teams.

People don't follow titles, they follow tone. And the tone you set during stress, conflict, and uncertainty will determine how your entire organization handles adversity.

This chapter is about mastering the hardest territory a leader will ever have to navigate: their own inner world.

The Emotional Landscape of Construction Leadership

Owning or running a construction business brings a complex emotional terrain. Some days you feel invincible—projects flowing smoothly, crews humming along, clients thrilled, numbers looking good. Other days it feels like everything hits at once.

Construction leadership brings its own emotional rhythm:

> **Stress**: The constant pressure to meet deadlines, keep budgets intact, and manage unexpected challenges can be overwhelming.

> **Frustration**: Delays, miscommunications, or issues with subcontractors can lead to feelings of irritation and frustration.

> **Pride**: There's a lot of pride in creating something tangible, whether it's a new building or a completed renovation. That sense of accomplishment is a huge emotional reward.

> **Anxiety**: Cash flow concerns, client complaints, and keeping the business afloat can cause anxiety, especially when you're just starting or dealing with a slow season.

> **Elation**: Successfully completing a project on time and within budget is one of the most satisfying moments in business ownership.

> **Disappointment**: Sometimes things won't go as planned. A misstep, an unexpected setback, or an unhappy client can create feelings of disappointment that may linger.

Loneliness

This emotion is rarely talked about, but nearly universal among owners. Everyone looks to you for answers, yet you rarely have a safe place to express the weight you're carrying.

Understanding that these emotions are normal and predictable gives you power. The goal isn't to eliminate emotion. The goal is to lead *through* emotion with clarity and composure.

Recognizing these emotions and acknowledging that they are part of the process is the first step to managing them effectively. You will inevitably face them, but how you respond makes all the difference.

Staying Grounded: The Importance of Perspective

As a construction business owner, it's easy to get caught up in the daily challenges and lose sight of the bigger picture. I know I had a tough time with this more often than not, it seemed. When a project hits a snag or a client is unhappy, it can feel like the end of the world. However, it's important to remind yourself that these obstacles are often temporary and that you have the experience and resources to work through them.

One of the best ways to stay grounded is to develop a strong sense of perspective. When you face a tough situation, ask yourself:

> ➤ **Is this challenge something I can fix, or do I need to delegate it?**
> ➤ **What can I learn from this setback?**
> ➤ **Will this issue matter in the long term, or will it be forgotten in a few months?**

Having a long-term vision for your business allows you to view setbacks as learning opportunities rather than insurmountable obstacles. This mindset helps you stay calm and focused during tough times, preventing emotional decisions that could harm your business.

Building Emotional Resilience

Resilience is the ability to bounce back from difficulties, and it's a crucial skill for any business owner, particularly in the unpredictable world of construction. This is one trait I do have. With all the challenges I faced as a business owner, bouncing back and finding the good was the best way for me to move on. But how do we measure resilience? As a coach, I use the **AQai** assessment to help owners and leaders develop a clear path and understand some of their emotions. Developing emotional resilience involves strengthening your ability to manage stress, adapt to challenges, and maintain your emotional well-being.

Here are some strategies to build emotional resilience:

Mindfulness Practices: Take time each day to check in with yourself and your emotions. Whether it's deep breathing, meditation, or simply taking a few moments of silence, these practices help center your thoughts and prevent stress from building up. Box Breathing worked for me. Breathe in through your nose, hold for 4 seconds, out through your mouth, hold for 4 seconds and repeat.

Self-Care: It's easy to overlook your own needs when you're running a business, but neglecting your physical and mental health can lead to burnout. Make time for regular exercise, healthy meals, and activities that help you relax and recharge. For me, this was waking up at 4:00 AM and getting a good workout followed by some time in the sauna.

> **Cultivate a Positive Mindset**: It's important to remain optimistic in the face of adversity. Reframing challenges as opportunities for growth or improvement helps you maintain a constructive mindset, even in difficult situations. To put it simply, make sure your glass is at least half full all the time!

> **Accept Imperfection**: The construction industry is messy and unpredictable. Accepting that things won't always go according to the plan helps reduce frustration and disappointment when things go wrong. Learn to embrace mistakes as part of the process.

Managing Emotional Triggers

Certain situations will naturally trigger emotional responses, tight deadlines, client complaints, conflicts with contractors, etc. Being able to recognize these triggers is a key part of managing your emotions effectively. Here are some techniques to help you handle these emotionally charged moments:

> **Pause Before Responding**: When you're upset or stressed, take a few moments to collect your

thoughts before responding. A deep breath or even a short walk can help you return to the situation with a clearer head. And for those crucial emails? Wait. Sleep on it if you can. We've all typed a long-winded email just to hit delete, delete, delete....

➢ **Use Clear, Calm Communication**: Often, conflict arises from miscommunication. When tensions are high, practice clear and respectful communication with your team, clients, and subcontractors. Calmly express your thoughts, listen actively, and work toward a mutually beneficial solution.

➢ **Delegate to Trusted Team Members**: You don't have to carry the emotional burden alone. If you're feeling overwhelmed by a particular issue, trust your team to take over certain responsibilities. Delegating tasks can reduce your emotional load and also empower your team members.

➢ **Seek Outside Support**: Whether it's a mentor, business coach, or therapist, having someone to talk to when you're struggling emotionally can provide invaluable perspective and emotional relief. Just remember you're the boss, so it's not a good idea to seek support below you in your organization.

Celebrating Successes (Big and Small)

Managing your emotions doesn't mean suppressing them. It's about finding balance and giving yourself the space to feel positive emotions, too. Make sure to celebrate your victories, no matter how small they may seem. Whether it's completing a project on time, securing a new client, or navigating a tough situation with grace, acknowledging these wins boosts your morale and reinforces the positive aspects of your work.

Celebration is also an important way to motivate your team and reinforce a positive work culture. When the team feels appreciated, they are more likely to stay motivated and handle stress effectively as well.

Conclusion

Managing your emotions as a construction business owner is a continual process that requires awareness, patience, and practice. By maintaining perspective, building emotional resilience, managing emotional triggers, and celebrating your successes, you can create a balanced, healthy environment for both you and your team. Running a construction business comes with its share of challenges, but when you approach those challenges with emotional clarity and resilience, you're better positioned to lead with confidence and navigate the ups and downs of the industry.

The most successful business owners aren't those who are immune to stress or setbacks; but those who know how to handle their emotions in a way that moves their business forward. Keep that in mind the next time you face a tough moment, and remember, you have the emotional tools to overcome it.

Emotional control is one of the most underrated leadership skills in construction, and one of the most powerful. When pressure hits, people don't watch what you say; they watch how you react. The ability to stay composed under fire earns respect, builds trust, and keeps teams grounded. Leadership isn't about suppressing emotion; it's about directing it toward clarity and courage.

Leadership Builder

Ask yourself:

> ➢ How do I respond under stress: react or reflect?
> ➢ What triggers derail my leadership presence, and how can I manage them better?
> ➢ How can I model emotional intelligence, so my team mirrors calm, not chaos?

Chapter 15

RAISING THE BAR: WHY THE SMARTEST LEADERS HIRE SMARTER

Building a Team that Elevates You

Strong leaders build teams that make them obsolete.

The strength of any organization, especially in the construction industry, lies in its people. Yet, one of the most common pitfalls for leaders is letting ego interfere with hiring decisions. A strong leader understands the importance of hiring individuals who are not just qualified but smarter, more skilled, and more innovative than they are in specific areas. This chapter delves into the importance of hiring smarter, how ego can derail the process, and strategies to build a team that elevates the entire organization.

Why Hiring Smarter is Crucial

Construction is a Team Effort

In construction, no single person can master every aspect of the job. A project's success relies on a cohesive team where members bring diverse skills and expertise. Hiring smarter ensures that every role, from site foreman to project manager, is filled by someone capable of handling complex challenges and making informed decisions. Specialists with deep knowledge in areas like engineering, safety, or technology can solve problems that others cannot.

Innovation Drives Success

The construction industry continues to evolve at a rapid pace, driven by advances in technology, sustainability, and project management. Staying competitive means surrounding yourself with people who embrace these innovations and know how to apply them in the field.

Hiring individuals who bring specialized skills—like a tech-savvy project manager proficient in BIM, GPS, or Total Station systems—can completely transform efficiency and accuracy. These tools streamline workflows, reduce costly rework, and reveal potential issues before they become real problems.

Years ago, while working for a civil utility and earthwork company, I experienced this firsthand. A project manager hired shortly before me was fresh out of college and highly skilled in GPS and 3D modeling software for takeoffs. His expertise was a game changer. For the first time, the company could visualize the entire project before breaking ground, spotting deficiencies, identifying conflicts, and saving both time and money. That single hire elevated the company's performance, proving that innovation isn't just about tools; it's about the people who know how to use them.

Strong Teams Reflect Strong Leadership

A leader who surrounds themselves with talented individuals demonstrates confidence and humility. This fosters a culture where growth, collaboration, and continuous improvement thrive.

The Ego Barrier

Fear of Being Outshined

Some leaders resist hiring individuals they perceive as more knowledgeable, fearing it might undermine their authority or make them seem less competent. Honestly, let's think this through: wouldn't your colleagues in the business world actually be impressed with what a good hire you made?

Overestimating Personal Abilities

Ego can lead leaders to believe they are the smartest person in the room, making them less likely to delegate or seek out expertise. I believe your job as a leader is to be the least important person in the room. If you are the least important person, then won't your business be running without you and generating income so you can put your time and effort into other ventures?

Resistance to Change

Ego-driven leaders may hire individuals who echo their opinions rather than those who bring fresh perspectives, limiting innovation and adaptability. This is where you find yourself continually on the hamster wheel running in circles doing the same thing.

How Ego Hurts Your Team

Stifling Growth

A team that lacks diversity in skillsets or thought processes becomes stagnant. Without smarter hires, the organization fails to evolve.

Undermining Morale

Employees may feel undervalued or micromanaged if leaders refuse to delegate or acknowledge their expertise. This can lead to disengagement and turnover.

Missed Opportunities

Refusing to hire individuals who bring greater expertise or fresh perspectives doesn't protect your position, it limits your company's potential. When leaders let ego or insecurity drive hiring decisions, they close the door on innovation, efficiency, and creative problem-solving. Every role left unfilled by someone smarter or more specialized is a missed opportunity for growth. Great leaders don't fear being outshined, they build teams that make the entire organization shine brighter.

Leadership Takeaway: *If you're the smartest person in the room, you've hired wrong.*

Leaders who embrace this mindset understand that growth comes from surrounding themselves with people who challenge the status quo. Hiring individuals with different strengths and perspectives pushes an organization to evolve. The construction industry, like any other, thrives on advancement, whether that's adopting new technology, improving safety practices, or optimizing project delivery. When leaders choose comfort over challenge, they stagnate. But when they choose curiosity, inviting in people who see things differently, they build a culture that never stops improving. The best leaders don't just hire talent; they create an environment where that talent can lead.

Benefits of Hiring Smarter Than You

Filling Knowledge Gaps

Strong leaders recognize what they don't know. Instead of viewing those gaps as weaknesses, they see them as opportunities to strengthen the team. Smart hires bring expertise in areas where the leader or organization lacks proficiency, whether it's technology, estimating, design, compliance, or communication. By filling those knowledge gaps intentionally, leaders transform blind spots into competitive advantages. When every role is filled by someone who knows their craft better than you do, your leadership focus shifts from doing to developing. You stop managing tasks and start leading people.

Encouraging Growth and Learning

Surrounding yourself with skilled individuals challenges everyone to elevate their game. High performers raise the standard for the entire team because excellence is contagious. When you bring in people who are passionate about what they do, they naturally pull others toward growth. This creates a culture of **continuous**

improvement, one where questions are encouraged, mistakes are viewed as learning moments, and curiosity is rewarded. Great leaders understand that the best teams are not built on compliance but on curiosity. The moment your team stops learning, your organization stops growing.

Encouraging growth also means creating space for it. Leaders who allow time for mentorship, training, and professional development don't just retain top talent, they build loyalty. When people feel valued and invested in, they invest back.

Enhancing Problem-Solving

When you hire people smarter than you, you don't just expand your technical capabilities, you expand your perspective. These individuals bring fresh ideas and challenge assumptions that may have gone unquestioned for years. They approach problems from angles you might never have considered, seeing opportunities where others see obstacles. Innovation doesn't happen in echo chambers; it thrives in diversity of thought.

Smart hires push you out of your comfort zone, and that's a good thing. They make you think differently, plan differently, and sometimes even lead differently. That friction, the creative tension between new ideas and old habits is where real progress happens.

Building a Resilient Organization

Ultimately, hiring smarter is about building **a team that thrives even when you're not in the room**. Resilient organizations are not dependent on a single leader's presence; they run on systems, trust, and empowered people. When you hire capable, forward-thinking individuals and equip them to lead, you create freedom: freedom for you to focus on strategy, to grow the business, or even to take that long-overdue vacation knowing your team has it handled.

A strong leader's goal isn't to be indispensable; it's to build a team. That's real leadership, creating a culture where excellence continues, progress compounds, and success sustains itself. Because when you hire smarter, you're not just filling positions, you're building legacy.

Strategies for Hiring Smarter

Define What You Need

Hiring smarter starts with clarity. Identify the specific skills, knowledge, and character traits that complement your existing team and fill current gaps in expertise.

> ➢ Assess where your organization struggles most, whether that's technology, communication, project management, or safety culture.
> ➢ Write job descriptions that emphasize problem-solving, adaptability, and innovation, not just technical ability.

Focus on Potential Over Familiarity

Hire for what someone *can become*, not just what they've done. Fresh perspectives often come from outside your industry. Someone from a technology or manufacturing background, for example, might introduce automation, digital tools, or new workflows that streamline construction processes. Hiring for potential invites innovation. Hiring for familiarity only reinforces the status quo.

Involve Others in the Hiring Process

No single person should carry the full weight of a hiring decision. The best teams are built through collective perspective. Inviting others into the interview process adds valuable insight and helps balance blind spots or personal bias. Each interviewer sees something different: attitude, technical ability, communication style, or cultural fit.

After interviews, take time to compare notes and discuss your impressions as a team. Patterns will emerge quickly, revealing not just a candidate's skills but their character and compatibility. This approach ensures you're evaluating from multiple angles, not just your own instincts. Collaboration in hiring doesn't weaken leadership, it strengthens it. It shows humility, values diversity of thought, and ultimately increases your odds of choosing someone who aligns with both your mission and your culture.

Ask the Right Questions

Great interviews uncover how a person thinks, not just what they know. Focus on problem-solving, critical thinking, and adaptability by asking questions such as:

> ➤ "Tell me about a time you solved a complex issue on a project."

> ➤ "How do you approach learning new technologies or systems?"
> ➤ "Describe a situation when you had to collaborate with someone whose approach was different from yours."

These questions reveal emotional intelligence, curiosity, and a candidate's ability to grow—qualities that matter far more than memorized answers or rehearsed achievements.

Check Your Biases

Be aware of the tendency to hire people who look, think, or act like you. Comfort can be costly. Diversity in thought, background, and experience fuels innovation and adaptability. The goal isn't to build a team of clones; it's to build a team of complements. Prioritize those who bring unique strengths to the table and who challenge you, respectfully, to see things differently.

When hiring smarter, remember: every addition to your team either amplifies or erodes your culture. The best leaders know how to hire for both competence and chemistry, ensuring that every new team member moves the organization forward, together.

Leading Without Ego

Once you've hired people who are smarter or more skilled in certain areas, your next responsibility is to trust them to do what you hired them to do. Great leaders delegate with confidence, not hesitation. Let your team take ownership of their roles and resist the urge to hover or correct every detail. Micromanagement kills initiative. Empowerment builds it.

Leadership without ego is also celebrating the success of others. When your people win, the company wins and so do you. Recognize their contributions publicly and genuinely. The best leaders make their teams feel seen, valued, and trusted. That kind of culture doesn't just improve performance; it inspires loyalty and pride.

Finally, shift your focus from being the "know-it-all" to being the visionary. Your job isn't to have all the answers; it's to ensure your people have what they need to find them. A construction CEO doesn't need to manage every foreman or oversee every GPS layout; they need to build a team that can. True leadership is stepping back so others can step up.

Because in the end, ego builds walls, trust builds leaders.

Overcoming the Fear of Being Outshined

Great leaders understand that when their team shines, it reflects their own success. Reframe what winning looks like. A team that excels isn't a threat to your authority; it's proof of your leadership. The best leaders build people who can perform at the highest level, even when they're not in the room.

Learn from your team. The smartest leaders stay curious. They see talented employees not as competition, but as teachers. Every new skill or idea your team brings to the table is an opportunity for you to grow alongside them. Humility isn't weakness, it's the doorway to continual improvement.

And most importantly, build a legacy. Your ultimate goal as a leader is to create a company and a culture that thrive long after you're gone. That requires hiring top talent, developing them relentlessly, and giving them space to lead. Success that depends on one person isn't sustainable, but success that's shared across a capable, empowered team will stand the test of time.

Your leadership is measured not by what happens while you're here, but by what continues when you're gone.

The Long-Term Impact of Smarter Hires

Hiring smarter than yourself doesn't just make your life easier, it shapes the future of your organization. The effects reach far beyond day-to-day operations and become part of your company's DNA. When you consistently bring in people who elevate the standard, you set in motion a ripple effect that transforms the entire culture.

Stronger teams emerge because high performers attract other high performers. Talented professionals want to work alongside others who challenge and inspire them. Before long, excellence becomes contagious, and mediocrity has no place to hide.

Innovation increases as diverse expertise and fresh perspectives collide. People from different backgrounds approach problems differently, leading to new ideas, streamlined processes, and smarter ways to build. When you surround yourself with people who think bigger than you, your company learns faster, adapts quicker, and grows stronger.

Sustainable growth follows naturally. A high-performing team doesn't depend on one leader's constant oversight, it runs on systems, trust, and shared accountability. That kind of team builds consistency, quality, and customer confidence. It's the difference between running a company that survives and leading one that lasts.

Leaders who hire smarter create an organization that doesn't just meet today's demands but anticipates tomorrow's challenges. Every smart hire compounds in value over time, creating depth, resilience, and a legacy of excellence. Because when you hire people who make the company better, you're not just building a team, you're building the future.

The smartest hire you'll ever make is the one who makes you better.

Conclusion

Great leaders understand that their success isn't defined by being the smartest person in the room, but by building a team of capable, innovative, and motivated individuals. By checking your ego at the door and hiring smarter than yourself, you create a foundation for growth, adaptability, and long-term success. In construction, where teamwork and expertise are paramount, the smartest decision you make is to surround yourself with people who challenge and inspire you. That's how you build not just great projects, but a great company with great leaders.

Insecure leaders hire followers; confident leaders hire thinkers. Great leadership means surrounding yourself with people who know more than you in their area of expertise. When you hire smarter, you're not replacing your value, you're multiplying it. The real measure of leadership isn't how many people depend on you, but how many grow because of you.

Leadership Builder

Ask yourself:

> ➢ Do I hire for comfort or for capability?
> ➢ Who on my team consistently challenges my thinking, and do I appreciate it?
> ➢ What traits define a "smarter than me" hire for my next position?

Chapter 16

THE GREAT UNKNOWN

Leading Through Change

Uncertainty doesn't destroy leaders; it defines them.

What does Adaptability mean to you? As a business owner in uncertain times, how do you adapt to ever-changing employees, technology, market share, and costs of doing business?

Adaptability and the Great Unknown in Construction

The construction industry is one of the most dynamic and unpredictable sectors, shaped by rapid technological advancements, evolving regulations, economic fluctuations, and environmental challenges. In this chapter, we explore the critical importance of adaptability in navigating the great unknowns of the construction world, offering insights into how industry professionals can thrive amid uncertainty.

Adaptability in Construction

Adaptability is the ability of construction professionals, project managers, architects, contractors, and workers to respond to changing circumstances. The nature of construction projects is inherently dynamic, with various unpredictable elements that require a flexible approach. There are several layers where adaptability is crucial:

➤ **Changing Client Needs**

Clients might change their minds during construction, whether about design elements, budget constraints, or timelines. This requires the project team to adjust to these new demands without sacrificing the overall project goals.

➤ **Regulatory Shifts**

Construction is heavily regulated, and codes or legal requirements can change during the lifespan of a project. Adaptable construction teams must quickly adjust to new laws or codes, especially in industries such as sustainability or safety.

➤ **Technological Advancements**

New tools, construction techniques, and technologies are constantly emerging. Teams must remain adaptable to incorporate these innovations into their projects, whether it's using drones for site surveying, BIM (Building Information Modeling) for design, or new materials that could improve the project's efficiency and sustainability.

➤ **Supply Chain Challenges**

Construction projects rely heavily on materials, and supply chain disruptions can have significant impacts. Whether it's price fluctuations, material shortages, or transportation delays, adaptability ensures teams can pivot to alternative solutions, such as finding new suppliers or adjusting project schedules.

> **Weather and Environmental Factors**
The weather can significantly impact the construction schedule. Unforeseen events like storms, flooding, or extreme temperatures can delay progress. Adaptive planning, such as having contingency schedules or utilizing climate-resilient materials, can help teams mitigate the impact.

Adapting to Changing Client Needs
(Strategic Growth & Client Alignment)

One of the most overlooked areas of adaptability isn't weather, regulation, or technology—it's client evolution.

When we were a smaller company, we had clients who were perfect for that stage of growth. We could meet and exceed their expectations. Our pricing structure worked. Our manpower model worked. Our availability aligned with their timelines. They were good clients, and we were grateful for them.

But as we evolved, as our systems matured, as we invested in better people, better equipment, stronger processes, and clearer direction, something started to shift. Some of those clients didn't evolve with us. It wasn't always about workload.

Sometimes it was price expectations rooted in who we used to be. Sometimes it was timing demands that no longer aligned with our scheduling model. Sometimes it was communication or scope creep that conflicted with the structure we were building. Servicing them became harder, not because they were bad clients, but because we were becoming a different company. That realization forced us to adapt.

We had to sit down and communicate clearly: "We value this relationship. We love working with you. But in order to keep our company functioning efficiently and delivering at the level we are committed to, we need to structure things differently." That meant adjusting pricing, setting firmer schedules, clarifying scope, and protecting our team's time and energy.

The risk was obvious: they could walk. And some did—some by design, some not. But what it created was space—space to pursue the type of work we saw ourselves doing in the future, to align with clients who valued our evolution, and to build toward the company we intended to become.

Adaptability sometimes means bending. Other times, it means redefining the playing field. If we try to hold onto every client from every stage of growth, we can unintentionally anchor ourselves to a version of the company we've already outgrown. The question becomes: Are you adapting to your clients in a way that strengthens your future, or in a way that traps you in your past? Growth requires clarity. Clarity requires courage. And courage sometimes means risking the loss of what once worked in order to build what will work next.

The Great Unknown in Construction

The "Great Unknown" in construction refers to the unpredictable aspects of a project that can't always be anticipated or planned for. It can manifest in several ways:

➢ **Unforeseen Site Conditions**

Excavating a site can uncover issues such as contaminated soil, hidden utility lines, or unstable ground conditions that weren't visible during the initial assessment. The "Great Unknown" here is that these problems weren't apparent in early planning and addressing them can require quick problem-solving and adjustments to the timeline and budget.

➢ **Cost Overruns**

Construction budgets are often subject to unexpected price increases or underestimations, particularly with long-term projects. For example, material prices might fluctuate, or labor costs might change unexpectedly. This uncertainty means project teams must have flexible financial strategies in place to deal with such volatility.

➢ **Project Complexity**

Each construction project is unique, and complexity often increases as projects involve multiple contractors, stakeholders, or complicated designs. The challenge is anticipating how these diverse elements will interact and evolve throughout the project lifecycle while managing unexpected conflicts and technical challenges that arise.

➢ **Human Factors**

Human factors, such as labor shortages, skills gaps, or interpersonal conflicts, are also part of the "Great Unknown." Even with the most well-planned projects, people remain unpredictable, and teams must adapt to any interpersonal challenges that might arise.

The Foreman Who Built Us, But Couldn't Lead Us Forward

(Human Factors & Organizational Adaptability)

Years ago, we hired a foreman who came with something powerful: influence. His two brothers worked for us. His dad worked for us. A couple of cousins worked for us. When he showed up, he didn't just bring experience; he brought a following.

At that stage in our company, he helped get us where we were. But as we began evolving, implementing systems, raising expectations, and shifting culture, it became clear that while he had helped build the foundation, he wasn't the right leader for where we were headed.

Letting him go wasn't just about one individual. It meant potentially losing seven. That winter was filled with fear. What if they all walked? What if we were short-handed in the spring rush? What if this decision crippled us? We made the decision anyway. And yes, we lost them.

But what we gained was far greater. Existing team members quietly thanked us. Morale improved. Accountability strengthened. We were able to pivot. We implemented changes that had been stalled. The culture shifted. Standards rose. The business matured.

That moment taught me something critical about adaptability and human factors: sometimes the "Great Unknown" isn't weather, pricing, or regulation. Sometimes it's people. Leadership isn't about avoiding loss. It's about protecting direction. He helped get us to where we were. But he wasn't going to get us to where we needed to be. Growth sometimes requires subtraction.

When Losing People is a Reset Button

(Resilience & Perspective in the Face of Workforce Loss)

Recently, a client of mine experienced something similar. A Project Manager quit. A few others followed. Suddenly, he felt exposed, understaffed, frustrated, and scrambling.

The instinct was to blame, to replay decisions, to point fingers. But I told him something he didn't expect: "This might be a blessing." Fortunately, his workload had softened slightly. The timing, while uncomfortable, was survivable. Instead of seeing loss, I challenged him to see opportunity. You just removed friction. You just cleared space. You just earned a reset.

We cannot control the past. We cannot rewrite it. But we absolutely control whether we allow it to define our future. Being a business owner is not easy. If it were, everyone would do it. It is precisely the changes and challenges—the uncomfortable exits, the staffing gaps, the unexpected departures—that force us to build stronger systems, refine hiring standards, clarify expectations, and improve culture.

Resilience is not pretending loss doesn't hurt. Resilience is choosing not to let it control you. The most adaptable leaders do not cling to what was. They ask: "What can this make possible?" Setbacks often create the space required to build something better.

Building Resilience Through Adaptability

Adaptability helps mitigate the risks posed by the great unknown in construction by enabling teams to pivot and solve problems in real time. Here are some strategies to build resilience:

> **Risk Management Plans**
>
> Proactively identifying potential risks is an important step toward adaptability. By having a solid risk management framework in place, construction teams can anticipate challenges such as weather delays, financial issues, and supply chain problems. Creating contingency plans helps teams remain agile when unexpected events occur.

> **Collaboration and Communication**
>
> Clear communication and collaboration between all stakeholders, architects, engineers, contractors, and clients are essential. A team that can quickly share information and adjust plans collectively is better equipped to deal with the unknowns that inevitably arise during a project.

> **Continuous Learning and Training**
>
> Given that construction is an industry that constantly evolves, ongoing training and development can help construction professionals stay ahead of emerging challenges. Whether it's learning about new software tools, construction methods, or compliance requirements, continuous education ensures teams can tackle unexpected changes efficiently.

➢ **Scenario Planning**
Being adaptable isn't just about responding to problems as they occur; it's also about preparing for a range of possible scenarios. Scenario planning involves considering a wide variety of outcomes and preparing strategies for each. This proactive mindset helps teams remain flexible when confronted with the unknown.

Embracing Change as a Constant

Construction projects often face unforeseen challenges, from sudden changes in client requirements to unexpected site conditions. Success in this industry hinges on an organization's ability to adapt to these variables without compromising quality, safety, or deadlines. Embracing change as a constant rather than an exception is a mindset shift that allows teams to remain resilient and proactive.

The Role of Technology in Adaptability

Technological innovation is transforming construction practices, offering tools to enhance adaptability. For instance:

➢ **Building Information Modeling (BIM):** Enables teams to simulate project outcomes, identify potential issues, and adjust designs in real time.
➢ **Drones and Robotics:** Provide real-time site data and improve efficiency in handling tasks under complex or hazardous conditions.

> ➤ **AI and Predictive Analytics:** Help forecast risks, material needs, and project timelines, empowering decision-makers to anticipate and mitigate challenges. Staying ahead of the curve with these technologies ensures that firms can adapt to both planned and unplanned changes efficiently.

Workforce Adaptability

Human adaptability is as crucial as technological flexibility. Construction workers and managers need to continuously update their skills to remain relevant. This includes embracing digital tools, adhering to new safety standards, and fostering interdisciplinary collaboration.

Training programs, mentorship, and a culture of lifelong learning can help build a workforce prepared for the unknown. Yet many companies lack in this area. How do you know if your teams are truly adaptable, and how do you measure it? How do you gauge whether your people feel confident and valued enough to share new ideas or technologies that could improve performance? Psychometric tools like the **AQai Adaptability Assessment** give leaders the data they need to answer those questions with confidence.

The assessment helps uncover each team member's unique strengths, stressors, and adaptability skills, giving you a clear view of where to focus your coaching. When you leverage strengths and develop weaknesses, teams become more open to change, more innovative, and more resilient. The real transformation begins when leaders apply what the assessment reveals, turning insight into action and adaptability into a daily habit.

Resilience in the Face of Environmental Challenges

Environmental uncertainties, such as extreme weather events and evolving sustainability mandates, are increasingly impacting construction. Adaptable practices, such as incorporating sustainable materials, implementing energy-efficient designs, and preparing contingency plans for weather delays, are essential to ensuring project continuity and minimizing environmental impact. For us, it was making sure we had rolls of plastic or burlap on hand in case Mother Nature threw a curveball.

Leveraging Agile Project Management

Traditional linear approaches to project management may struggle to handle the unknowns of modern construction. Agile methodologies, which emphasize flexibility, collaboration, and iterative problem-solving, allow teams to respond quickly to changes. Regular feedback loops, stakeholder engagement, and adaptive planning ensure smoother project execution even in uncertain conditions.

Agile isn't just a project management framework; it's a mindset shift. In construction, this means moving away from rigid plans that crumble under change and instead building systems that flex and respond in real time. Agile encourages **short, focused cycles of planning and execution**. Think of it as running a series of "mini-projects" within a larger build.

Each cycle ends with a review, feedback, and adjustment before the next phase begins. This keeps communication clear, risk visible, and accountability shared across teams. When combined with leadership that values transparency and collaboration, Agile transforms chaos into coordination. It empowers crews to make informed decisions in the field, adapt to evolving conditions, and maintain momentum even when uncertainty hits.

Just as Agile teams adapt their plans, **leaders must adapt their leadership**. The same principles that drive an Agile project, iteration, feedback, and flexibility, apply to people. Great leaders regularly assess what's working, listen to their teams, and adjust their approach instead of clinging to a fixed style. This doesn't mean abandoning structure; it means building responsiveness into it.

When leaders model adaptability, they create a psychological safety environment where team members feel valued enough to share concerns, propose innovations, and take ownership of solutions. In a world where change is constant, **the most adaptable leader sets the pace for the most adaptable team.**

The Competitive Edge of Adaptability

In a competitive industry, adaptability is not just a survival strategy but a competitive advantage. Firms that can pivot quickly in response to market demands, regulatory changes, or technological advancements are better positioned to seize opportunities and mitigate risks.

Conclusion

The construction industry **operates at the intersection of innovation and unpredictability**. By fostering a culture of adaptability through embracing technology, equipping the workforce, and implementing flexible management practices, construction professionals can confidently navigate the great unknown and build a resilient future.

Change is constant in our industry: shifting markets, evolving safety standards, supply issues, new technologies, and the workforce. Adaptability separates survivors from innovators. Great leaders stay steady in uncertainty, using vision and communication to steer through volatility. They model resilience so others don't fear change; they learn to thrive in it.

Leadership Builder

Ask yourself:

- How do I personally respond to uncertainty, with fear or with focus?
- What systems or habits keep my team agile when plans fall apart?
- How can I lead with confidence when the path ahead isn't clear?

Section Three

KILLING THE CULTURE KILLERS

Chapter 17

CONTAGIOUS CULTURE

Getting Rid of the Negative Before It Spreads

Negativity spreads faster than any safety meeting or morning huddle.

In the hot, dusty, and sometimes dirty world of construction, a single negative influence can quickly disrupt team morale, efficiency, and overall project success. Just like rust on steel or cracks in a foundation, negativity can weaken even the strongest organizations if left unchecked. This chapter explores how negativity manifests, why it spreads so easily, and actionable strategies to identify and address it before it causes lasting damage.

The Cost of Negativity

Negativity isn't just a morale killer, it directly impacts productivity, safety, and the bottom line.

Reduced Morale and Engagement

A negative attitude can quickly demoralize even the most motivated employees, leading to disengagement and decreased effort.

Example: A foreman who constantly criticizes their team without offering constructive feedback can cause resentment and lower morale across the crew.

Lower Productivity

Negativity distracts employees from their work, slowing progress and increasing the likelihood of errors.

Safety Hazards

In construction, distractions caused by negativity can lead to unsafe behavior or accidents. When your head isn't in the game, you become complacent.

Increased Turnover

Employees are less likely to stay in a toxic environment, which can lead to high turnover, recruitment costs, and loss of institutional knowledge. This will ultimately affect your bottom line. As we discussed earlier, employee turnover can cost upwards of $10,000. Think of the Monday Blues, those employees who dread coming to work on Mondays eventually quit coming.

How Negativity Spreads

Negativity often spreads faster than positivity, as it thrives on emotions like frustration and fear.

Gossip and Rumors

A single disgruntled employee spreading rumors can create distrust and division among the team.

Passive–Aggressive Behavior

Unspoken resentment or subtle undermining can create a toxic undercurrent that's hard to detect, but damaging over time.

Resistance to Change

Negative attitudes toward new policies, tools, or leadership can cause widespread reluctance and delay progress.

Example: A group of employees resisting the adoption of new technology might influence others to reject it before giving it a fair chance, thus ultimately costing the company time and money.

Identifying Negativity

Warning Signs

Be vigilant for early signs of negativity:

- ➢ Increased complaints or blame-shifting.
- ➢ Decline in teamwork or collaboration.
- ➢ High absenteeism or disengagement.
- ➢ Verbal and non-verbal cues, such as sarcasm or eye-rolling during meetings.
- ➢ Someone scoffing when confronted.

Sources of Negativity

Determine whether negativity stems from individuals, team dynamics, or external factors. Common sources include:

- ➢ **Toxic employees**: Individuals who consistently bring down the morale of others.
- ➢ **Poor leadership**: Lack of communication, favoritism, or unfair treatment.
- ➢ **Unrealistic expectations**: Pushing teams too hard without proper resources or recognition.

Patrick Lencioni, in his book *Silos, Politics, and Turf Wars*, explores one of the most common barriers to organizational health, division. Think about your own company for a moment. Do silos exist within your teams? Groups or cliques that just can't seem to find a way to work together?

Now take that reflection a step further. Are there teams you naturally favor over others? People under your leadership you find difficult to connect with, or maybe even can't stand? Every organization struggles with this to some degree. The challenge for a leader is to recognize it, confront it, and build bridges instead of barriers.

When silos go unaddressed, they become fertile ground for **negativity**. Resentment grows, communication breaks down, and "us versus them" thinking begins to take hold. It starts small, a sarcastic comment here, a dismissive attitude there, but it spreads quickly. Before long, those silos become echo chambers where complaints replace collaboration and blame replaces accountability.

Negativity feeds on separation. The less teams interact, the easier it is for assumptions, rumors, and frustration to take root. The cure isn't another meeting; it's intentional leadership. Breaking down silos means creating environments where people are seen, heard, and valued beyond their role or department. Because when connection increases, negativity loses its power to divide.

Strategies to Address Negativity

Confront the Issue Directly

Address negativity as soon as it's identified. Avoid letting it fester.

Steps to Take:

➢ Speak privately with the individual or group involved.

➢ Listen to their concerns and validate any legitimate frustrations.

➢ Provide clear feedback on how their behavior impacts the team and the company.

Set the Tone as a Leader

Leadership sets the culture of the workplace. Demonstrating positivity, fairness, and respect encourages employees to follow suit.

➢ Avoid engaging in gossip or favoritism.

➢ Be consistent in your actions and communication.

➢ Show empathy and appreciation for your team.

Foster Open Communication

Create an environment where employees feel comfortable expressing concerns constructively rather than letting frustrations simmer.

➢ Hold regular team check-ins or toolbox talks to discuss challenges and progress.

➢ Encourage feedback and solutions rather than complaints.

> Act on valid concerns to show employees their voices matter.

Remove Toxic Employees if Necessary

While coaching and support can help most employees turn their behavior around, some individuals may refuse to change.

Example: A consistently disruptive employee who undermines leadership and refuses coaching may need to be let go to protect the team's overall health.

Promote Positivity and Teamwork

Combat negativity by creating a workplace culture that rewards positive behavior and collaboration.

> Recognize and reward team accomplishments.
> Encourage mentorship and peer support.
> Provide training in conflict resolution and effective communication.

Preventing Negativity in the Long Term

Hire the Right People

Prevent negativity from entering your organization by hiring individuals who align with your company's values and culture.

> Use behavioral interview questions to assess attitude and teamwork skills.
> Check references to ensure candidates have a track record of positive contributions.

Set Clear Expectations

From the outset, communicate expectations for behavior, teamwork, and professionalism. Make it clear that negativity and toxic behavior will not be tolerated.

Build a Resilient Culture

Create a culture that values resilience, adaptability, and mutual support. Teams with strong bonds and shared goals are less susceptible to negativity.

One of the best ways to stop negativity before it starts is during the hiring process. Culture begins with who you let through the door. We talked about this a few chapters before (Chapter 15): when interviewing, don't make it a solo effort, **cross-interview**. Compare notes with others who have met the candidate and build on what they've already uncovered. Ask deeper, follow-up questions that reveal how the person communicates, collaborates, and handles conflict. This layered approach not only provides a fuller picture of the candidate but also helps you spot potential red flags early. A strong résumé may prove skill, but cross-interviewing ensures a stronger fit, someone who will strengthen your culture, not divide it.

The Ripple Effect of Eliminating Negativity

From Ripple to Root: Stopping Negativity Before it Starts

Eliminating negativity doesn't just lift morale, it transforms performance, safety, and relationships. But to make that change last, leaders have to look deeper than surface symptoms. Negativity rarely starts with one event; it starts with one person, one attitude, or one unchecked behavior that spreads quietly through the crew. Often, it begins where teams are divided, inside the silos that form when departments, foremen, or even leadership stop communicating and start protecting their own turf. Patrick Lencioni calls this out in *Silos, Politics, and Turf Wars*, describing how division can poison an organization from the inside out.

When silos exist, frustration follows. Communication turns defensive, teams lose trust, and small conflicts turn into cultural cracks. To build a healthy organization, leaders must actively bridge those gaps, not just react when they appear. That means fostering connection, building understanding across teams, and even tightening up the hiring process to prevent negativity from entering in the first place.

When negativity is addressed and eliminated, the benefits extend beyond just morale:

> **Higher productivity**: Teams work more efficiently and with fewer distractions.

> **Better safety records**: Employees focus on their tasks without the added stress of a toxic environment.

> **Improved retention**: Employees are more likely to stay in a positive, supportive workplace.

> **Stronger client relationships**: Happy, motivated teams deliver higher-quality results, earning client trust and loyalty.

Conclusion

Negativity is a silent threat to any construction project or organization, but it doesn't have to take root. By identifying and addressing it early, fostering open communication, and creating a culture of positivity, leaders can protect their teams and projects from its harmful effects. Eliminating negativity isn't just about solving a problem, it's about building a stronger, more resilient team that thrives in even the toughest conditions. Remember, in construction as in life, the foundation you lay determines the structure's strength. Get rid of the negativity before it spreads, and your team will stand stronger than ever.

Every crew, company, and culture is built on the behaviors leaders tolerate. The moment you allow negativity to take root, complaining, blaming, gossip, or poor attitude, you start losing good people. Great leaders don't ignore negativity; they confront it early, consistently, and with empathy. **Your culture is either being built intentionally or infected passively.**

Leadership Builder

Ask yourself:

- ➤ Where am I tolerating negativity in the name of "keeping the peace?"
- ➤ How quickly do I address toxic behavior before it damages morale?
- ➤ How can I reinforce positive behaviors publicly while correcting negative ones privately?

Chapter 18

CUSTOMER EXPERIENCE

How Negative Culture Destroys Reputation

A client once told me something that stuck with me for years. We were wrapping up a project when he pulled me aside in his driveway and said, "You know what I noticed? Your people act the same way in front of me as they do when they think I'm not around."

He meant it as a compliment. And it was. But the truth behind that simple observation reached deeper than either of us discussed in that moment.

Customers always notice the culture behind the work, whether you think they see it or not.

- ➤ A crew that respects each other will respect clients.
- ➤ A team that communicates openly will communicate with clients.
- ➤ A company that values its people creates employees who value their customers.

Clients feel the culture long before they ever comment on quality. Long before they sign a contract, approve a change order, or write a check, they silently form an impression, not about your craftsmanship, but about the character, consistency, and cohesion of your people.

The customer experience doesn't begin with the handshake.

It begins with your culture.

Customer Experience versus Customer Service

You'll notice I call it *Customer Experience* instead of *Customer Service*. That's intentional. Customer service is reactive; it responds when something happens. Customer experience is proactive; it shapes how someone feels throughout the entire relationship.

In construction, the customer experience is shaped by everything: the professionalism of your crews, the clarity of your communication, the decisions your team makes when no one is looking, the pride they bring to their work, and even the tone of your jobsite meetings. Clients not only buy the product; they buy the feeling that comes from working with you.

A great customer experience creates loyalty. A poor one creates doubt. And doubt is devastating in an industry built on trust.

The Critical Role of Customer Experience in Construction

Construction isn't like most industries. Our work interrupts people's lives, affects their schedules, impacts their budgets, and requires them to place enormous trust in a company's competence and character. Because of that, the customer experience is not a moment, it's a journey.

It begins in the planning phase, where clients judge your

responsiveness, your transparency, and your ability to listen. It continues during construction, where they evaluate how you communicate, how you handle challenges, and how your crews behave on-site. And it lasts well beyond project completion, because clients remember how you handled them when things got tough, not just when things went right.

Clear communication anchors this journey. Clients want to know what's happening, why it's happening, and what comes next. When the unexpected happens, and in construction it always does, the way your team explains, responds, and reassures makes all the difference.

Problem-solving is equally essential. Clients don't expect perfection; they expect leadership. They want to see your team take ownership, find solutions, and collaborate with professionalism.

And reliability ties the entire experience together. Delivering on your promises, whether a timeline, a budget, or a commitment, builds the trust that keeps clients coming back.

When these elements work together, you build a reputation that carries more weight than any marketing campaign. When they don't, relationships fracture, and even small issues begin to feel like major red flags.

How Negative Culture Damages the Customer Experience

Culture is the invisible engine behind every interaction your company has with its clients. When the culture inside is toxic, disengaged, or strained, the effects ripple outward.

Low morale is often the first internal sign of external trouble. Employees who feel undervalued are less likely to show enthusiasm, compassion, or urgency. They complete tasks; but they don't take ownership. The pride that drives great customer experiences is replaced by fatigue or frustration.

Communication breaks down next. In unhealthy cultures, employees often avoid speaking up, sharing concerns, or asking questions. Internally, this leads to confusion, missed details, and friction between teams. Externally, clients receive unclear updates, slow responses, or sugar-coated information that erodes trust.

Accountability becomes scattered. When people fear blame or criticism, they deflect responsibility. Problems linger instead of being solved. From the client's perspective, it feels like no one is steering the ship, and nothing damages confidence faster.

Turnover intensifies these issues. As experienced team members leave, clients sense the instability. They find themselves working with new faces who lack the history or context of the project. Continuity is lost, and trust becomes fragile.

And perhaps most damaging, negative cultures resist change. They cling to old practices, avoid improvement, and stop innovation. In a fast-moving industry, clients quickly notice when a company operates with outdated processes or rigid attitudes.

In short, culture drives experience. And the wrong culture drives clients away.

The Domino Effect of Negativity

Imagine a firm where leadership dismisses ideas, the atmosphere is tense, and stress is the norm. In this kind of environment, the dominoes fall quickly.

On the jobsite, workers begin cutting corners, not out of laziness but because engagement has vanished. Details get missed. Safety habits weaken. Work quality becomes inconsistent.

Project managers hesitate to communicate honest challenges to clients. Instead of confronting issues early, they avoid tough conversations. Problems escalate when they could have been prevented.

Client-facing staff deliver updates without enthusiasm or empathy. They offer the bare minimum because that's all they have left to give.

What began as internal dysfunction eventually becomes external disappointment. Clients don't need to see what happens inside your company; they feel it.

And once they feel it, they start looking elsewhere.

Building a Culture That Elevates the Customer Experience

Improving customer experience starts with improving the employee experience. People treat clients with the same energy they receive from leadership.

When employees feel engaged, appreciated, and supported, they naturally raise the level of customer care. They communicate better. They solve problems faster. They take pride in doing things right the first time.

Leadership plays a central role here. When leaders model transparency, the team becomes more honest. When leaders give credit and recognition, the team gives more effort. When leaders hold themselves accountable, accountability spreads.

Training reinforces this culture. Employees who understand your values, your expectations, and your vision can confidently communicate that to clients. And when teams have the right tools, knowledge, and processes, they serve clients with greater clarity and professionalism.

Alignment keeps everything moving in the right direction. When every employee knows how their role impacts the client relationship, they show up differently. They understand that the customer experience isn't just the responsibility of the PM or the superintendent, it's everyone's responsibility.

As culture strengthens, celebrate the wins. Share client feedback. Highlight outstanding service moments. Positivity creates more positivity.

The Payoff: A Reputation That Works for You

A strong internal culture doesn't just improve the customer experience; it builds a reputation that attracts the right clients and keeps them coming back. Clients feel the enthusiasm. They feel the pride. They feel the consistency and professionalism.

As your culture strengthens, two things happen:

> ➢ Your people stay longer, and your clients stay longer.
> ➢ That combination turns a construction company into a legacy.

Conclusion: The Customer Experience

The truth is simple: customer service begins on the inside. You cannot expect your crews to deliver excellence externally if they're frustrated internally. Negative culture doesn't just hurt retention; it erodes reputation. And reputation, once damaged, is hard to repair.

At its core, customer experience is an emotional connection. People do business with people they trust. When you show genuine interest not just in their project, but in their lives, their families, their passions, you build relationships that outlast contracts.

Some of my best client relationships were forged not on job walk-throughs or budget meetings, but far from the jobsite on fishing trips in the Florida Keys, or salmon runs on Lake Michigan with my friend Captain Nick Scaffidi of Milwaukee Offshore Fishing. Those experiences created stories and friendships that will outlive every project we completed.

Richard Weylman captured this truth beautifully in his book *100 Proven Ways to Acquire and Keep Clients for Life*. When I heard him speak at a PBCA conference, it confirmed something I had always believed:

The best customer experience isn't something you deliver.

It's something you share.

Leadership Builder

Ask yourself:

> ➢ How does the way my team treats each other reflect how they treat our customers?
> ➢ What part of our customer experience is most influenced by company culture?
> ➢ How can I model gratitude and professionalism with every client contact?

Chapter 19

MICROMANAGEMENT

How it Stifles Leadership & Growth

Control feels safe, but it silently kills initiative.

Micromanagement is one of the most common and most damaging leadership behaviors in any industry, but its effects are especially visible in construction, where momentum, autonomy, and on-the-fly decision-making are crucial to progress. Leaders often justify their involvement as protection, protection of quality, protection of outcomes, protection of their reputation. Yet what feels like protection slowly becomes restriction. And restriction, when left unchecked, turns into an invisible ceiling no one on the team can rise above.

A coach of mine once told me, "Don't be the funnel." At first, I brushed it off, but over time the truth in that simple phrase hit me hard. When you are the funnel, everything, every decision, every approval, every step, must flow through you. Nothing moves unless you touch it. Nothing progresses unless you respond. Nothing succeeds unless you confirm it. And if you're honest with yourself, running a business is hard enough. Do you truly want to do it all?

Micromanagement starves organizations of independence and starves leaders of freedom. It appears helpful in the short term but quietly destroys the long-term potential of a company and its people. To understand how to eliminate it, you must understand what it really is, not just the behaviors but the mindset beneath them.

Understanding Micromanagement

Micromanagement is not simply paying attention. It is not accountability. And it certainly is not leadership. Micromanagement is a pattern of over-involvement in tasks, decisions, and processes that should be owned by someone else. It's the instinct to hover, correct, override, and control. It's the inability to trust someone to follow through without your direct, constant input.

You can see it in the way a leader shadows an employee's work and tells them exactly how every detail "should be done." You see it when a leader refuses to delegate important tasks because deep down, they don't believe anyone else will meet their standard. You see it when decisions made by capable employees are reversed without conversation or justification, replaced by the all-too-familiar phrase, "Just do it my way." You see it when a leader demands constant updates on minor details that do not require their attention. And you see it clearly when a leader expects perfection not just in outcome but in process, believing every step must mirror their own.

Micromanagement sometimes masquerades as thoroughness. But thoroughness equips people. Micromanagement undermines them.

It also erodes accountability. Leaders think they are

being responsible by inserting themselves everywhere, but the opposite is true. When employees aren't allowed to make decisions, they cannot be held responsible for outcomes. Ownership travels upward until one person ends up carrying the weight of every decision, every problem, every project. And when that happens, the organization no longer functions as a team, it functions as an extension of a single leader's anxiety.

The Hidden Damage Micromanagement Creates

Micromanagement has an immediate emotional cost. People who feel constantly watched or corrected eventually stop believing in their own capability. They withdraw. They stop offering ideas. Their confidence disintegrates because they know their leader will step in anyway. When employees lose autonomy, they lose engagement, and when they lose engagement, morale drops quickly.

Turnover follows not far behind. High performers, the people you most want to keep, will not stay in an environment that restricts their growth. When professionals feel suffocated or undervalued, they find somewhere else to contribute their talent.

Productivity also suffers. When a leader inserts themselves into every task, progress slows to the speed of that leader's availability. Decisions that should take minutes take hours. Tasks that should move forward stall because permission hasn't been granted. The team stops thinking. They stop acting. They simply wait.

The decline in innovation is even more subtle. In cultures dominated by control, employees learn to stay quiet. They avoid proposing solutions because they've learned their ideas will be overridden. Creativity fades. Initiative dies. And the company begins operating in survival mode instead of growth mode.

The irony is that while the team becomes less productive, the micromanaging leader becomes more overwhelmed. They end up carrying the responsibilities of an entire department instead of building people capable of carrying the load. Over time, exhaustion sets in. When you try to run every part of the business, you eventually run yourself into the ground.

Trust, once broken, becomes the hardest thing to repair. Employees begin to believe that leadership does not trust them, so why should they trust the leadership? Collaboration deteriorates. Communication becomes guarded. People feel they need permission to breathe. And culture becomes transactional instead of transformational.

In the end, micromanagement does something even more damaging: it prevents the business from scaling. A company cannot grow if one person needs to touch everything. There are only so many hours in a day, and only so much decision-making capacity in one mind. To grow, you must multiply yourself, not duplicate your workload.

Why Leaders Micromanage

Micromanagement often comes from fear: the fear of failure, of mistakes, of something slipping through the cracks.

It also comes from perfectionism, where leaders believe their way is the only right way, even when others have the competence to do the job. Sometimes it comes from the lack of trust, whether justified or not.

It can come from insecurity, as well. New leaders, unsure of their authority, overcompensate with control. Others adopt micromanagement simply because it was modeled for them; they don't know another way.

And often, it comes from short-term thinking. Taking control in the moment seems faster, easier, or more efficient. But the long-term cost is enormous.

The first step in overcoming micromanagement is recognizing the root beneath the behavior. Leaders who understand *why* they micromanage can finally begin to elevate beyond it.

Breaking the Cycle of Micromanagement

Releasing control is not an overnight transformation; it is a series of intentional choices. It begins with delegation, not as a task dump but as a development strategy. Delegation says, "I trust you. I believe in your ability. I'm giving you ownership because I want you to grow."

It continues with shifting focus to the big picture, strategy, culture, processes, vision. Leaders who escape the weeds finally create space for their organization to evolve.

Trust is another essential step. Trust grows each time you allow someone to make a decision without correction. It grows when you let them own a process, solve a problem, or experiment with a different approach. Trust doesn't appear spontaneously; it is built through opportunity.

Training and support help too. People can't thrive if they aren't equipped, and leaders can't release control if they don't believe their team is prepared. When you invest in training, you invest in freedom.

Clarity provides a foundation. When people know what success looks like, they don't need you hovering over each step. They can move forward with confidence, knowing the target and owning the path to reach it.

A growth mindset transforms mistakes from failures into learning opportunities. Leaders who embrace this mindset elevate both themselves and their teams, leaving perfectionism behind in exchange for progress.

And self-awareness, the humility to reflect, adjust, and change, is the thread that ties everything together. Leaders who can examine their own behavior with honesty become the leaders who evolve the fastest.

A Story from the Field

I once worked with a company where one person made every decision. This individual determined crew locations, assigned jobsite tasks, approved materials, solved every conflict, decided what to bid, and directed every next step. Project managers existed in title only; every decision they attempted to make was overridden.

The team felt powerless. The company moved slowly. Deadlines slipped because no one felt authorized to act. Innovation disappeared. Morale dropped. And eventually, turnover increased because talented people refused to stay confined to the sidelines.

Only when the leader stepped back and allowed project managers to lead did the organization begin to heal. With delegation came ownership. With ownership came action. With action came growth.

The issue had never been the team.

It had been the leader's inability to release control.

The True Cost of Micromanagement, and the Freedom of Letting Go

Micromanagement is not leadership. It is fear disguised as authority. It signals insecurity, erodes trust, and suffocates creativity. True leaders do not hover, they equip, empower, and step back. They give their teams room to think, experiment, and solve problems. They allow others to shine.

When you trust people to make decisions, something powerful happens:

➢ They start thinking like leaders.
➢ The more control you release, the more influence you gain.
➢ And the more you empower others, the more your organization and your people thrive.

Leadership Builder

Ask yourself:

➢ What am I micromanaging out of fear instead of leading through trust?

> How can I shift from checking up on people to checking in with them?
> What would happen if I let my team make one more decision without my approval?

Chapter 20

BROKEN BEFORE YOU BEGIN

Why Reactive Leadership Fails

Leaders who only fix what's broken will always stay broken themselves.

In construction, where precision, planning, and efficiency are essential, the philosophy of "drive it 'til the wheels fall off and put new wheels on" can have catastrophic consequences. This mindset, which implies running equipment, processes, or teams into the ground and fixing them only after they fail, prioritizes short-term gains over long-term sustainability. While it may seem like a way to save time or money, this approach often results in higher costs, lower productivity, and irreparable damage to morale and reputation.

What Does "Drive it 'Til the Wheels Fall Off" Mean?

This phrase refers to a reactive approach to management and operations, characterized by:

➢ **Neglecting Maintenance:** Running machinery, equipment, or systems until they break rather than proactively maintaining them.

> **Overworking Teams:** Pushing employees to their limits without considering their physical or mental well-being.
> **Ignoring Warning Signs:** Dismissing early indicators of problems in favor of continuing at full speed.
> **Delaying Investments:** Postponing upgrades or replacements for tools, equipment, or systems until failure is unavoidable.

While it may appear resourceful in the short term, this approach is unsustainable and often leads to significant operational and financial setbacks.

Leadership Insight: The Parallel Between Iron and Integrity

Every piece of equipment on a jobsite tells a story about leadership. The backhoe that's greased regularly, the truck that's inspected weekly, and the crew that feels seen and supported, all reflect the same mindset: respect for what drives production. Reactive leadership wears things down; proactive leadership builds things up.

Neglecting maintenance is no different than neglecting mentorship. Overworking people mirrors over-revving machines, eventually, both seize. The best leaders know that longevity, safety, and efficiency start with stewardship, not speed.

Why This Approach is Detrimental

1. Equipment:

> **Increased Downtime**
> Equipment failures and breakdowns result in unexpected downtime, disrupting project timelines.

Repairs or replacements often take longer than routine maintenance, further delaying progress.

➢ Higher Costs

Emergency repairs and unplanned replacements are typically more expensive than preventative measures.

Frequent breakdowns can lead to overtime pay, expedited shipping for parts, and lost revenue.

2. Human Capital:

➢ Reduced Productivity

Teams are less efficient when working with unreliable equipment or in a disorganized environment.

Stress and frustration caused by repeated failures diminish overall productivity.

➢ Safety Hazards

Operating worn-out machinery or pushing teams to exhaustion increases the likelihood of accidents and injuries.

Failing to address safety concerns can lead to regulatory violations and costly legal consequences.

➢ Employee Burnout and Turnover

Overworking employees without addressing their needs leads to burnout, dissatisfaction, and resignations.

A work environment where problems are constantly "put out" rather than prevented creates stress and frustration for employees. Workers become disengaged, affecting overall productivity and retention.

High turnover disrupts operations, increases hiring costs, and diminishes team cohesion.

3. The Organization:

➢ **Damage to Reputation**

Consistent delays, safety incidents, and poor-quality outcomes damage relationships with clients and stakeholders.

A reputation for neglect and inefficiency makes it harder to secure future contracts.

Clients notice delays, breakdowns, and poor performance. Once trust is lost, it's difficult to regain, leading to lost contracts or fewer referrals.

Why Organizations Fall into This Trap

➢ **Short-Term Focus**

Pressure to meet deadlines or stay within tight budgets can lead to neglect of long-term priorities.

➢ **Lack of Planning**

Inadequate planning and resource allocation results in reactive rather than proactive decision-making.

➢ **Lack of Data and Transparency**

Without clear systems to track maintenance schedules, employee well-being, and project performance, decision-makers may not fully grasp the consequences of neglect until it's too late.

➢ **Underestimating Consequences**

Leaders may not fully understand the long-term

impact of neglecting maintenance, upgrades, or employee well-being.

> **Budget Constraints**

Many construction firms operate on tight budgets where immediate cost savings take precedence over long-term planning. Leaders might delay equipment maintenance or upgrades, viewing them as an expendable line item until a breakdown forces action.

> **Cultural Inertia**

In organizations where this mentality has persisted for years, it becomes normalized. Employees and leaders alike adapt to a "just get it done" culture, even if it means ignoring best practices.

From Reactive to Proactive: The Leadership Shift

Reactive Leadership says:

> "We'll fix it when it breaks."
> "We'll deal with it when it happens."
> "We don't have time for that right now."

Proactive Leadership says:

> "We'll prevent it from breaking."
> "Let's fix the cause, not the symptom."
> "Let's build a plan before it becomes a problem."

Leaders who plan ahead build sustainability. Those who constantly react create chaos. The same is true for every system, equipment maintenance, safety planning, budgeting, or culture. Preventative leadership is about anticipating friction points and addressing them before they become fires.

The Better Alternative: Proactive Management

Let's examine how proactive practices in specific areas can mitigate the risks of this mindset:

> **Preventative Maintenance**
>
> Implement digital asset management systems to track maintenance schedules, equipment usage, and potential breakdowns.
>
> Schedule downtime for maintenance during off-peak hours to minimize disruption.

> **Invest in Quality**
>
> Prioritize high-quality materials, equipment, and tools that offer durability and reliability.
>
> Upgrade outdated systems or machinery before they fail, reducing the risk of costly downtime.

> **Workforce Well-Being**
>
> Invest in programs that monitor employee workloads, prevent burnout, and offer support. This can include mental health resources, flexible scheduling, and regular check-ins.
>
> Recognize and reward employees who identify and solve small issues before they become major problems.

> **Risk Management**
>
> Conduct regular audits of processes, equipment, and safety measures.

Use predictive analytics to forecast potential risks, allowing the organization to address issues before they escalate.

➤ **Long-Term Planning**

Shift the focus from short-term fixes to long-term solutions that support sustainable growth.

Align organizational goals with strategies that balance efficiency, quality, and safety.

➤ **Training and Development**

Equip employees with the skills and knowledge to recognize early warning signs, whether it's a machine showing signs of wear or a process that isn't working efficiently.

Offer cross-training so employees can step in and keep operations running smoothly if others are unavailable.

➤ **Client Relations**

Be transparent with clients about the importance of proactive planning and how it benefits them. For example, explain how routine maintenance minimizes project delays.

Involve clients in long-term planning discussions to align expectations with sustainable practices.

Overcoming Resistance to Change

Shifting away from this mindset requires addressing resistance within the organization. Changes won't and don't have to happen all at once or overnight, but they may need to happen—and one by one is how to get it done.

Here are some ideas to help your organization:

- ➢ **Cultural Buy-In:**
  Highlight success stories where proactive planning led to positive outcomes. Show how these changes benefit everyone, from top management to field workers.

- ➢ **Small, Incremental Changes:**
  Start by implementing proactive measures in one area, such as maintenance schedules or employee wellness, then scale them gradually.

- ➢ **Data-Driven Decision-Making:**
  Use data to demonstrate the cost-effectiveness of proactive measures. For example, compare the costs of routine maintenance versus emergency repairs to make a compelling case for change.

- ➢ **Empowering Employees:**
  Encourage employees to take ownership of their workspace, equipment, and processes. Empower them to report small issues before they escalate.

Amazon's Approach to Near-Miss Reporting:

A Lesson in Proactive Safety

Even with one of the most complex operational systems on the planet, Amazon understands the value of catching problems before they become incidents. Through programs like its Dragonfly near-miss reporting system, employees can quickly report near-misses, potential hazards, or safety concerns using digital tools located throughout their facilities. These reports feed directly into a continuous improvement process designed to identify risks, analyze patterns, and implement corrective actions before injuries occur.

What makes this approach notable isn't the technology; it's the mindset. Amazon's safety system aligns with international standards, emphasizing prevention, worker participation, and data-driven improvement. Employees are encouraged to speak up through multiple channels: mobile reporting, safety committees, anonymous boards, and direct feedback sessions. The focus is not on blame or paperwork, but on learning. Every close call becomes a data point for improvement, a small win in preventing something bigger down the road.

For leaders in construction, mining, and manufacturing, the takeaway is clear: a strong near-miss culture is one of the best investments you can make. When workers feel empowered to report hazards without fear of reprisal, you shift from reactive leadership, fixing what's already broken, to proactive leadership, preventing the break in the first place. Whether you use a high-tech app or a simple paper card on the job trailer wall, the goal is the same: make it easy to speak up, close the loop on every report, and build trust through consistent follow-up.

Real World Consequences:

Example: A construction firm adhered to the "drive it 'til the wheels fall off" mentality, delaying maintenance for heavy machinery to save costs. As a result:

A critical piece of equipment broke down in the middle of a large project, causing weeks of delays.

Emergency repairs and rental equipment costs exceeded the budget by 30%. Employee morale dropped as workers faced extended hours to make up for lost time.

Example Contrast: A competing firm implemented proactive maintenance and employee wellness programs. Their projects consistently stayed on schedule, their teams were motivated, and they gained a reputation for reliability and professionalism, securing repeat business.

The Long-Term Benefits of Proactive Practices

- **Cost Savings:** Preventative measures reduce the need for costly repairs, overtime pay, and replacement parts.
- **Improved Efficiency:** Well-maintained equipment and motivated employees operate at peak productivity.
- **Enhanced Safety:** Regular inspections and attention to employee well-being minimize safety risks.
- **Stronger Reputation:** Clients value reliability, professionalism, and a commitment to quality, leading to repeat business and referrals.
- **Sustainable Growth:** A proactive approach builds a foundation for scalability and long-term success.

Leadership Through Stewardship

True leadership is stewardship of people, equipment, and purpose. The leader's job is to ensure the organization runs efficiently, safely, and sustainably. That means scheduling downtime before downtime schedules you. It means balancing productivity with protection.

When a leader respects the tools and teams that make the work possible, that respect multiplies. Crews take ownership. Equipment lasts longer. Clients notice consistency. Reputation becomes reliability and reliability becomes revenue.

> **The Role of Leadership:**
> To move away from the "run it into the ground" mentality, leadership must play an active role in fostering change. This requires a mindset shift and an intentional focus on long-term sustainability.

> **Vision and Values Alignment:**
> Leaders must prioritize sustainability, quality, and safety as core organizational values. By aligning decisions with these principles, they create a culture of proactive planning rather than reactive problem-solving.

> **Lead by Example:**
> When leaders prioritize preventative measures, like maintenance schedules, realistic project timelines, or employee wellness, it sets a standard for the entire organization.

> **Communication and Transparency:**
> Clear communication is essential to help employees understand the "why" behind changes. For instance, explaining how routine equipment maintenance

prevents delays, fosters buy-in from workers who might otherwise see it as downtime.

Recap of Preventive Leadership Practices

1. Plan Maintenance Like a Project. Treat every maintenance window as an investment in uptime, not an interruption.
2. Equip the Team, Don't Exhaust Them. Monitor workloads and morale just like engine hours. Rotate tasks, rest crews, and reward foresight.
3. Track Data, Not Damage. Use digital tools to monitor maintenance schedules, productivity trends, and safety indicators. Lead with visibility.
4. Communicate the "why." When crews understand how proactive steps prevent bigger problems, they buy in.
5. Celebrate Prevention. Recognize those who catch issues early; it builds a culture where speaking up equals leadership.

"Drive it 'til the wheels fall off" is a short-sighted approach that sacrifices sustainability for immediate results. In construction, where precision and efficiency are critical, this mentality leads to higher costs, diminished productivity, and weakened relationships. The same pattern shows up in organizations across every industry, even those operating at massive scale.

Whether you're managing a jobsite or a global supply network, the principle remains the same: leadership that waits for things to break is already broken. The road to success is not paved with quick fixes but with foresight, planning, and a commitment to doing things right. Because in leadership, as in construction, the cost of neglect is always greater than the price of prevention.

The Leader's Role: From Operator to Guardian

A strong leader doesn't just drive performance, they guard it. They view equipment, people, and systems as assets to protect, not expendables to consume. Preventive leadership transforms "drive it 'til it breaks" into "maintain it, so it thrives."

When leaders embrace this mindset, projects flow smoother, safety improves, and turnover declines. Most importantly, it demonstrates maturity, the kind of leadership that's measured not by how fast you move, but by how long you last.

Leadership Builder

Ask yourself:

- ➤ Am I running my people or equipment too hard in the name of productivity?
- ➤ How can I build proactive maintenance, mechanical *and* cultural, into my leadership routines?
- ➤ What one system, habit, or piece of equipment could benefit most from preventive attention this month?
- ➤ How can I model "maintenance mindset" so my team mirrors it?

Chapter 21

THE COST OF MOTION

When "Keeping the Crews Busy" Builds More Problems Than Profit

Motion doesn't always mean progress.

In the construction industry, downtime for crews is often viewed as an expensive liability. As a result, many companies fall into the trap of taking on work solely to keep their crews busy, regardless of its profitability or strategic alignment. While this approach may appear to prevent immediate losses, it can lead to long-term inefficiencies, financial strain, and organizational decline. This chapter explores why "keeping the crews busy" is a flawed strategy and how to implement more sustainable practices for long-term success.

The Appeal of "Keeping the Crews Busy"

➢ **Avoiding Idle Costs**

Idle crews cost money, from wages to equipment rentals, without generating revenue. Managers often scramble to fill these gaps with any available work, believing that any revenue is better than none.

➢ **Maintaining Team Morale**

Some leaders think keeping crews active will boost morale by ensuring employees feel productive and valued.

- ➤ **Preserving Skills and Workflow**
  Regular work helps maintain team momentum and ensures employees stay sharp and ready for larger projects.
- ➤ **Fear of Losing Talent**
  When employees are not consistently engaged, they may look for work elsewhere, leaving gaps in the workforce.

These seem like the right thing to do when the phone isn't ringing, or you haven't gotten work lately. Yet, while these motivations seem reasonable, they often overlook the broader implications of prioritizing activity over strategy.

The Hidden Costs of Working Just to Stay Busy

- ➤ **Unprofitable Projects Drain Resources**
  Taking on low-margin or loss-making projects consumes time, labor, and materials that could be reserved for more profitable opportunities.

  Over time, this erodes cash flow and puts the organization in financial jeopardy.
- ➤ **Increased Wear and Tear**
  Performing unnecessary or inefficient work accelerates equipment wear and tear, leading to higher maintenance and replacement costs. Essentially you are making no money on equipment utilization.
- ➤ **Employee Burnout**
  Keeping crews constantly busy, especially with

unproductive or uninspiring tasks, leads to burnout and disengagement.

Employees may begin to question leadership decisions, reducing trust and morale.

➤ **Opportunity Costs**

Resources tied up in low-value projects cannot be redirected to high-margin or strategically significant work.

The organization may miss out on larger, more profitable projects because crews and equipment are already committed.

➤ **Reputation Damage**

Accepting subpar work or delivering poor-quality results due to rushed or ill-considered projects can damage your reputation with clients and stakeholders.

➤ **Stifled Innovation**

A focus on staying busy leaves little room for strategic planning, skill development, or adopting new technologies.

How This Strategy Leads to Organizational Decline

➤ **Erosion of Profit Margins**

Consistently taking on unprofitable work creates a financial deficit that can spiral out of control.

This leaves the organization vulnerable to economic downturns or unexpected expenses.

- **Loss of Strategic Direction**

  Over time, the focus shifts from long-term goals to short-term fixes, weakening the organization's competitive edge.

- **Employee Turnover**

  Burnout, dissatisfaction, and a lack of meaningful work can drive employees to seek opportunities elsewhere, leaving the organization understaffed.

- **Compromised Quality**

  Crews working on poorly planned or rushed projects are more likely to make mistakes, leading to rework and damaged client relationships.

- **Diminished Client Trust**

  Taking on work for the sake of staying busy often results in poor communication, missed deadlines, and inconsistent quality—eroding trust and reducing repeat business.

Breaking the Cycle: What to Do Instead

- **Prioritize Quality Over Quantity**

  Focus on securing fewer, high-quality projects with strong profit margins.

  Turn down work that does not align with your strategic or financial goals, even if it means short-term downtime.

- **Invest in Training and Development**

  Use downtime to upskill employees, provide safety training, or introduce new technologies.

This ensures crews are more capable and efficient when high-value projects arise.

➤ **Proactive Project Pipeline Management**

Develop a robust pipeline of future projects to reduce downtime and maintain steady revenue.

Build relationships with clients to secure repeat business and referrals.

➤ **Focus on Efficiency**

Improve workflows and processes to reduce costs and maximize profitability on each project.

Evaluate equipment utilization and maintenance to ensure resources are used effectively.

➤ **Adopt a Strategic Reserve Mindset**

Treat idle time as an opportunity to prepare for upcoming opportunities rather than a liability to avoid.

Reserve crews and resources for high-margin projects that align with long-term goals.

➤ **Strengthen Financial Planning**

Maintain a financial buffer to absorb the costs of occasional downtime without resorting to unprofitable work.

Analyze profit margins and operational costs to identify areas for improvement.

Example: The Pitfalls of Staying Busy

A construction firm adopted a "keep the crews busy" approach, taking on small, low-margin projects between larger contracts. While this temporarily reduced downtime, the long-term consequences included:

> A 20% increase in equipment repair costs due to overuse on unnecessary tasks.
> Lower morale among employees, who felt their skills were underutilized.
> Missed opportunities to bid on larger, more profitable projects because resources were tied up.
> Financial losses on small projects that barely covered operating expenses.

In contrast, when the company shifted its focus to proactive planning and strategic project selection:

> Profit margins improved as the company focused on high-value contracts.
> Employee satisfaction increased with better training and more meaningful work.
> The firm built a reputation for reliability and quality, securing repeat business and referrals.

The Long-Term Benefits of Strategic Work Allocation

By abandoning the "keep busy" mindset and adopting a strategic approach, organizations can:

> **Increase Profitability:** Focus on projects that align with financial goals, ensuring sustainable growth.
> **Enhance Employee Engagement:** Empower crews

with meaningful, well-planned work that aligns with their skills and career goals.

➢ **Strengthen Client Relationships:** Deliver consistent quality and reliability, building trust and loyalty.

➢ **Foster Innovation:** Use downtime to explore new technologies, improve workflows, and develop skills.

➢ **Achieve Organizational Resilience:** Maintain a healthy financial position and a flexible workforce capable of adapting to changing demands.

Conclusion

Taking work just to keep the crews busy is a short-sighted strategy that can erode profitability, morale, and the overall health of your organization. Instead, focus on long-term planning, strategic project selection, and proactive resource management. By prioritizing quality, efficiency, and sustainability, you can build a resilient organization that thrives even during challenging times. The key to success isn't filling every hour with work, it's ensuring that every hour contributes to your goals and growth.

Filling the calendar just to stay busy is one of the easiest traps for construction leaders to fall into. It feels productive, but it often hides inefficiency. When you take on the wrong work just to keep crews moving, you burn resources and morale. Great leaders slow down long enough to choose wisely. Every project should move the company closer to its mission, not just fill the week.

Leadership Builder

Ask yourself:

- ➤ Do the jobs we take align with our long-term goals, or just short-term survival?
- ➤ How can I train my team to value strategic work over constant activity?
- ➤ Where am I confusing busyness for effectiveness in my own leadership?

BONUS CHAPTER

Chapter 22

THE 19TH HOLE

Where the lessons of the fairway meet the realities of the jobsite

For many in construction, golf plays a pivotal role, from benefit outings and association events to building client relationships and creating new business connections.

Being a contractor here in the Midwest, I used to wonder why we'd give up a perfect day of work to play a game that involves swinging a club over 100 miles an hour at a ball barely an inch and a half wide. What could go wrong, right?

As I began building a strong team, those golf events became a normal part of my business life. I wish I could say my game improved with time, it didn't. But the more I played, the more I loved it.

Golf wasn't new to me. My dad managed golf courses across the Midwest, and I grew up in the Junior PGA program at whatever country club he happened to be running. Fast forward to adulthood, and at times I still looked like that same eight-year-old kid out there hacking away.

What I've realized over time is that golf, much like business, demands focus, consistency, and patience. You can't force results. You can only refine your process and trust it. My local golf pro, Nate, reminds me of that constantly: *trust the process.*

That simple advice applies to more than just your swing. Many business owners struggle because they don't trust the process. They don't give time for new systems to work. They revert to the "legacy" ways that got them into trouble in the first place.

So, from the words of my golf pro and echoed by every great business coach I've ever known: *"Trust. The. Process."*

How Golf is Like Running a Construction Company

At first glance, golf and running a construction company may seem worlds apart. One is a sport rooted in precision, patience, and strategy; while the other is a fast-paced, high-stakes industry requiring coordination, problem-solving, and execution. But upon closer inspection, the parallels are striking. Both demand a combination of skill, adaptability, and focus, where every decision can significantly impact the outcome. Just like a golf game, running a construction company isn't about rushing to the finish line; it's about playing smart, thinking ahead, and mastering the details while keeping your eyes on the bigger picture.

The Course: Navigating the Challenges

In golf, each course presents unique challenges like water hazards, bunkers, and rough terrain that test even the most seasoned players. Similarly, in construction, every project comes with its own set of obstacles: tight budgets, shifting timelines, unexpected site conditions, and demanding clients. Success in both requires the ability to analyze the situation, anticipate challenges, and develop a clear plan to navigate them. A golfer doesn't simply swing wildly and hope for the best, they study the course, choose the right club, and visualize the shot. In construction, the same principle applies; thoughtful planning, resource allocation, and preparation are critical to overcoming challenges and delivering a successful project.

The Clubs: Choosing the Right Tools

A golfer's bag is filled with a variety of clubs; each designed for a specific purpose. Choosing the wrong club for a particular shot can spell disaster. The same is true in construction, where selecting the right tools, equipment, and methods can make or break a project. Leaders in construction must understand the strengths and limitations of their resources, be it the crew, materials, or technology, and deploy them strategically to maximize efficiency and minimize risks. Just as a golfer must adapt to changing conditions on the course, construction leaders must be flexible and responsive to the unpredictable nature of projects.

The Swing: Precision and Consistency

In golf, a consistent and precise swing is the foundation of success. One miscalculated swing can send the ball off course, requiring extra strokes to recover. In construction, consistency in processes, communication, and execution is equally important. A single mistake—whether a misaligned measurement, overlooked detail, or missed deadline—can set a project back significantly, impacting timelines and budgets. Both golf and construction teach the value of refining your technique, learning from mistakes, and striving for consistency to achieve the best possible results. I read somewhere: forward progress is best, and when playing golf, all you must do is improve over your last game. Shoot for one stroke less and then as you continue to do this, you find yourself getting closer to your goals, and this holds true whether it's golf or construction. Seems like a no-brainer, right? Small steps equal huge success.

The Mental Game: Staying Focused Under Pressure

Golf is as much a mental game as it is a physical one. Players must stay calm, focused, and confident under pressure, especially when faced with difficult shots or high-stakes tournaments. Similarly, construction leaders often operate in high-pressure environments, juggling competing priorities, tight deadlines, and unexpected challenges. Both pursuits require emotional intelligence, resilience, and the ability to make sound decisions under stress. Leaders who can stay composed and think strategically in challenging situations will consistently outperform those who react impulsively or let emotions dictate their actions. Have you ever gone to the course to play a round with your buddies, but realized you must have left your mind at work? It's happened to me plenty of times. You find yourself thinking about a big job that is in bidding process, or you have an employee issue at the top of your mind. This is why most professional sports teams train their players on how to handle stress and stay focused to perform their best.

The Team: Collaboration and Support

While golf is often seen as an individual sport, professional golfers rely heavily on their caddies for advice, perspective, and support. In construction, no leader can succeed without a strong and cohesive team. A great construction leader, like a skilled golfer, knows how to rely on their team, delegate tasks effectively, and trust their experts whether it's project managers, engineers, or field crews. Just as a caddie helps a golfer see the bigger picture and weigh options, a strong team helps construction leaders make informed decisions and execute their vision.

The Long Game: Patience and Strategy

Both golf and construction require a focus on the long game. Success isn't achieved in a single swing or a single project, it's the result of careful planning, strategic decision-making, and consistent effort over time. In golf, you may have a bad hole, but the round isn't over. In construction, a project might face setbacks, but how you recover and move forward defines your success. Both demand the ability to learn from mistakes, stay focused on the end goal, and maintain a steady, strategic approach.

The 19th Hole: Celebrating Success

Finally, golf and construction share the importance of celebrating achievements. In golf, the 19th hole, or the clubhouse, is where players reflect on their performance, share stories, and build camaraderie. In construction, celebrating project milestones and successes fosters team morale, strengthens relationships, and reinforces a culture of excellence. Recognizing accomplishments, both big and small, keeps teams motivated and focused on the next challenge.

Conclusion

Running a construction company is, in many ways, like playing a round of golf. Both require skill, strategy, patience, and adaptability. They demand that you navigate challenges, make calculated decisions, and focus on long-term success rather than quick wins. Whether on the golf course or a construction site, those who master the art of planning, precision, and resilience will find themselves on a winning path. So, as you take on the challenges of running your construction company, remember: every swing counts, every choice matters, and the game isn't over until the final putt. Play smart, lead with intention, and enjoy the journey, because much like golf, the joy of construction lies in mastering the process and celebrating the wins along the way.

Great golfers and great leaders know: the goal isn't perfection; it's consistent improvement and self-discipline.

Leadership Takeaway:
Leadership requires the same patience, rhythm, and focus as golf. The more you practice emotional control and precision, the better you perform under pressure.

In both golf and business, the scorecard doesn't lie. It reveals where you're consistent, where you're careless, and where you're improving, if you're willing to look honestly.

Leadership Builder

Ask yourself:

> ➢ What "bad shot" in leadership have I learned most from?
>
> ➢ How can I slow my pace and think strategically before reacting?

CLOSING–BUILDING BEYOND THE BLUEPRINT

When the last slab is poured and the jobsite falls quiet, leadership is what remains standing.

Leadership: The Framework That Holds It All Together

As we bring this book to a close, I want to leave you with a powerful reminder: the construction industry is, at its core, a *people-driven business*. I once had a coach tell me, *"You're not in the construction business, you're in the people business."* He was right.

Yes, the equipment, materials, and contracts matter; but they are only as strong as the people who operate them. It's your team, your leaders, and *you* who ultimately determine whether a company just survives or truly thrives.

The lessons in these chapters were designed to help you build a business that does more than generate profit; they help you build one that generates pride. One where people feel valued, trusted, and empowered to bring their best selves to work every single day.

Leadership is the foundation. Everything else, safety, quality, culture, and profit, sits on top of it.

The Power of Leadership and Communication

Leadership in construction isn't about barking orders from the pickup window; it's about building belief. It's the ability to create a vision, communicate it clearly, and inspire others to make it real.

As we explored, leadership grows through coaching, influence, and empowerment, not authority alone. When you connect your "why" to your crew's purpose, you create alignment. Alignment builds ownership. Ownership builds excellence.

Communication is where this leadership comes alive. The best leaders meet people where they are, listen before they speak, and translate complex goals into clear direction. When communication improves, performance also improves. Frustration fades, collaboration grows, and suddenly, the jobsite starts to hum like a well-tuned engine.

Leadership Takeaway:

Communication is not a task on the to-do list—it's the bridge that carries vision into action.

Operational Excellence: The Backbone of Growth

Leadership sets the direction, but operations provide the structure. Systems and SOPs, clear roles and responsibilities, and measurable KPIs give your team the clarity they need to perform.

When you define processes, you remove confusion. When you document expectations, you remove excuses. When you empower your team through structure, you create freedom within framework.

As you implement the strategies covered in this book, the 5% Challenge, proactive maintenance, smarter hiring, and trust-based delegation, you'll see more than efficiency. You'll see confidence, accountability, and pride take root across your company.

Leadership Takeaway:
Great leaders don't just design systems, they design ownership.

Culture: The Deciding Factor

Culture is what happens when leadership walks off the jobsite.

If your people continue to do the right thing, treat each other with respect, and take pride in their work even when you're not watching, you've succeeded. But if negativity, micromanagement, or burnout begin to creep in, the culture will crumble, no matter how strong the systems are.

Toxic culture spreads silently, draining motivation, damaging client trust, and pushing away your best people. The cure is intentional leadership: removing negativity before it spreads, rewarding initiative, and creating an environment where people feel seen and supported.

Because at the end of the day, it's not concrete, steel, or contracts that build companies. It's *culture*.

Leadership Takeaway:
Culture is the reflection of leadership when no one's looking.

The Path Forward

Now you hold the blueprint. The next step is to build.

Growth doesn't come from reading; it comes from applying. Don't try to fix everything at once. Start small. Choose one process to document, one habit to change, one conversation to have. Lead the first meeting differently. Listen more. Coach deeper.

Each action, no matter how small, moves your company toward greater stability and strength.

Remember: investing in your people is not an expense; it's the smartest, most profitable decision you can make. A well-led, well-trained, and well-supported team will always outperform one that feels undervalued or unheard.

Leadership Takeaway:
The most valuable asset in your company isn't your fleet, it's your people.

Lead the Legacy

Every project ends but leadership doesn't. The lessons you've learned in this book aren't temporary, they're transferable.

The next generation of leaders is watching you right now. They're learning how to lead by watching *how you lead*. Your tone, your patience, your integrity, it all leaves a mark.

So build something bigger than a business. Build a *legacy*. A company that leads with purpose, communicates with clarity, and never sacrifices its people for production.

The future of your company is not written in concrete; it's written in character.

Forge leaders. Build culture. Lead with purpose

That's how you build beyond the blueprint.

Leadership Builder (Closing Reflection)

Ask yourself:

➢ What legacy am I building through my leadership every day?

➢ How can I create more leaders, not just more followers?

➢ What will my team say about my leadership when I'm no longer in the room or on the site?